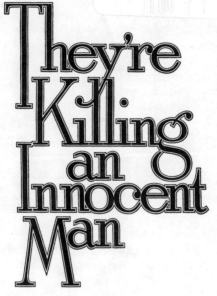

They're Killing an Innocent Man

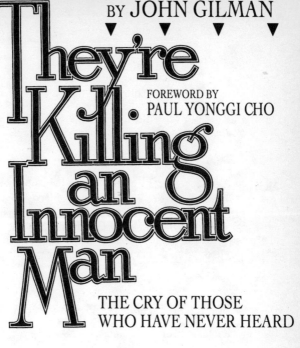

BY JOHN GILMAN

▼ ▼ ▼ ▼

They're Killing an Innocent Man

FOREWORD BY
PAUL YONGGI CHO

THE CRY OF THOSE
WHO HAVE NEVER HEARD

WORD PUBLISHING
Word (UK) Ltd
Milton Keynes, England
WORD AUSTRALIA
Kilsyth, Victoria, Australia
WORD COMMUNICATIONS LTD
Vancouver, B.C., Canada
STRUIK CHRISTIAN BOOKS (PTY) LTD
Maitland, South Africa
CHRISTIAN MARKETING NEW ZEALAND LTD
Havelock North, New Zealand
JENSCO LTD
Hong Kong
JOINT DISTRIBUTORS SINGAPORE –
ALBY COMMERCIAL ENTERPRISES PTE LTD
and
CAMPUS CRUSADE
SALVATION BOOK CENTRE
Malaysia

THEY'RE KILLING AN INNOCENT MAN

Copyright © 1991 by John Gilman.

First published in the USA by Creation House, a division of Strang Communications Company, Lake Mary, Florida.

Word (UK) Ltd edition 1992.

ISBN 0-85009-568-9   (Australia ISBN 1-86258-219-X)

Unless otherwise noted, all Scripture quotations are from the New King James Version of the Bible. Copyright © 1979, 1980, 1982 by Thomas Nelson Inc., publishers. Used by permission.

Scripture quotations marked KJV are from the King James Version of the Bible.

The Scripture quotation marked 'Moffatt' is from the Moffatt Bible. Copyright © 1976 by Harper Collins Publishers. Used by permission.

Printed and bound in Great Britain for Word (UK) Ltd. by Cox & Wyman Ltd., Reading.

92 93 94 95 / 10 9 8 7 6 5 4 3 2 1

DEDICATION

Eight days before Donald A. McGavran died of bone marrow cancer at the age of 94, I recorded a sacred conversation I had with Dr. McGavran, considered by many to be the world's foremost missiologist.

I wanted to see him again in person to ask several urgent questions. "You better come out here quick," he explained. "I might be gone in thirty days." Only four months earlier Mary Elizabeth, his dear wife of sixty-eight years, had preceded him to heaven's throne room. I knew from his voice he was about to step into eternity.

"Dr. McGavran," I began, with the utmost respect, "you have served God in India for thirty-six years; you are founder of the School of World Missions at Fuller Theological Seminary; you were born of missionary parents, actually a third-generation missionary yourself. You are called the father of the modern church growth movement. Now you are about to leave the field of harvest." My heart was full of admiration and love as I continued, "What would you like to say to those of us who share your vision? What final exhortation would you give as you pass the baton to us?"

The answer to that question is what this book is all about. I gladly dedicate this humble effort to his memory and pledge to honor his request.

As you read this book, may you be blessed to see beyond the inspiration and emotion of what has been written to that which made Donald A. McGavran one of this century's greatest Christian leaders. And may you take up the challenge to which he gave his entire life.

Many people, both from the past and the present, have inspired this dramatic story by their examples and ideas.

First, I am eternally grateful to my associates, the brave national workers who have often risked their lives to share the gospel in their native lands. Second, I am thankful to the many friends of the ministry, without whose loving prayer and support nothing could have been accomplished. And third, I am thankful for the invaluable influence I have received through the writings and personal fellowship with many contemporaries working in the harvest field.

I am especially indebted to M.G. (Pat) Robertson for giving me an opportunity to share in one of this century's greatest Christian endeavors, the development of Christian television. His personal example of faith and courage, his uncompromising loyalty to God's Word and his friendship have done more to encourage me than I could ever put in writing.

I wish to thank my dad for that monumental decision he made to follow Christ when I was a boy and for how he chose to model those old-fashioned virtues of honesty, loyalty and hard work. I give special honor to my dear deceased mother for demonstrating that the severest suffering can become just a thorn to pin aside the veil that hides the face of Christ, and for her prayers that have surely followed me the whole world through.

And I cannot possibly tell how my wife and partner, Caroline, from the days we first met in the ninth grade more than thirty-four years ago, has given her life totally for mine, and most of all, for Christ. I thank her for her practical wisdom and courage and her unswerving confidence throughout this exciting but often trying journey. I must also thank my sons, John and Stephen, for always being sensitive and concerned, making parenting truly a great joy.

CONTENTS

A cry is rising from every continent and every island, from every nation and every city, from palaces and from filthy ghettos: It's the cry of those who have never heard that God sent His Son to deliver them from sin.

Do you ever feel overwhelmed when you think of the task of the Great Commission? Christ has commanded us to tell the whole world! But we do not need to be overwhelmed because the Holy Spirit will show us how — by placing His dreams and visions in our hearts.

I started my ministry in 1958 in the slums of Seoul, Korea, right after the Korean conflict. The people were in a miserable condition, without even enough to eat. I bought an old tent and preached constantly — to five people.

Then I felt the flaming visions of God in my heart. The Holy Spirit showed me a church of three thousand members. So when I would stand before my church of five people on Sunday, I preached at the top of my voice as if I were preaching for three thousand.

Those five people came to me and told me I should not speak in such a loud voice. They said, "You hurt our ears. You are only speaking to five persons. Why do you speak so loudly?"

In the human realm I was in the tent church with five persons, but in the Holy Spirit realm I was seeing an entirely different situation.

Many people think you are going to make the visions and dreams, but the visions and dreams are going to make you. The Holy Spirit began by making me a pastor of three thousand. And by 1964 I was preaching to three thousand people in a beautiful church building. I was so excited that the dream had come to pass. I was satisfied. Why should I ask for more?

But when you are comfortable, the Holy Spirit will not work. The Holy Spirit takes you out of your comfortableness. He said to me, "If you can believe for ten thousand, then I will give you ten thousand."

Then the Holy Spirit, the master architect, built the visions and dreams in my heart again. I began to see ten thousand people.

By 1969 we had eighteen thousand members in our church.

The cycle of visions and fulfillment continued. The Holy Spirit stretched my vision to thirty thousand, to one hundred thousand, to three hundred thousand, to a million people.

So far we have seven hundred thousand members. In three years we'll have one million members, because every month we are receiving more than ten thousand new converts into our church.

Why do I tell you my life story of visions and dreams? God has given John Gilman a vision to use film to evangelize the world in a new way. Just as with me, the Holy Spirit is revealing His plan to John step-by-step. First He gave him a vision for producing a film of the life of Christ for the people of India. But this would not be a film of white faces and Western ways. It would be a film that was relevant to the Indian culture. That vision was fulfilled by a film produced with Indian actors. Then a new vision exploded in his thoughts again. He watched audiences of Indians weep over the scene of the crucifixion of Christ, and he dreamed of taking the film to all the villages in India, to show them the gospel in a way they could readily understand and to lead them to salvation through native evangelists.

For the past ten years, Dayspring International has been building such a ministry in India. And now their vision is expanding again. They yearn to make more films with native actors in Africa and China, to touch more of the world that is beyond the reach of the printed word, television or radios.

As you read this story, praise God for what He is going to do in the world through indigenous film evangelism. And when you pray, remember that God wants to put His dream and His vision in your own heart, so that you too can win people for Jesus.

Paul Yonggi Cho
Seoul, Korea

ONE

A SMALL DROP
OF WATER

Stop! Please stop now!"

The taxi driver could speak little English, but he knew what I meant.

What I had just seen on that sultry afternoon in a noisy, palm-leafed village near India's Bay of Bengal brought my life to an abrupt halt. All at once I felt joy, resentment, curiosity, excitement, even betrayal.

Suddenly the babble of the street vendors with their *cire-perdue* bronzes and their *dhokra* toy animals was beyond my hearing. The smell of crisp golden *jelabis*, dripping with syrup, held no interest. The colorful saris of saffron and indigo faded from view.

Before me was a larger-than-life billboard with a scene I never expected to see — especially in this Hindu-dominated land. There was Jesus, with the crown of thorns piercing His brow, blood flowing down His face, struggling to carry a huge wooden cross. Behind Him were the faces of what seemed like millions of Indian people.

Immediately I realized the billboard was promoting a major motion picture of the life of Christ. In Hindi the title of the film was *Daya Sagar* [pronounced DIE-uh SAW-guh].

"What do those words mean in English?" I asked until I found the answer.

"Oceans of mercy" was the reply.

"O Lord," I cried, "have I come halfway around the world to bring the message of Jesus through motion pictures — only to find it's already been done?"

Questions

It was February 1979. I had just resigned from my position as an executive producer of the Christian Broadcasting Network — an awesome ministry in which the Lord had allowed me to participate. My wife, Caroline, and I had sold our home and risked our entire future to follow God's call and vision. This was my second trip to India in just three months. To me there was no question that I was to produce a film that would reach millions for Christ. But now this!

I looked up and said, "Lord, why didn't You tell me? Am I wasting all my efforts?" I became frightened and confused. It seemed that my whole life was a preparation for making such a film.

On a scrap of paper I wrote the name of the movie house where the film was playing. I rushed back to the home of a missionary friend who spoke the language and said, "We're going to the movies tonight." I had to see it immediately.

As we made our way into the theater, dozens of questions filled my mind. Was I going to see a perversion of the gospel? Could an Indian film company really tell the story of Jesus? Had some missionary organization "stolen" the dream God had given me?

Over two thousand people jammed the cinema that night. That isn't a huge crowd by Indian standards. Movies play an important role in the nation's life-style; they provide an escape from the grinding poverty. More than three million people every *day* buy inexpensive movie tickets, making it the most dominant form of entertainment. More than six hundred films are produced each year in many of India's fifteen official languages, providing full-time employment for over 300,000 people.

On my first trip to the subcontinent I spent untold hours watching local films, analyzing their production, trying to find a strategy for the dream the Lord had planted and nurtured in my heart.

Tonight, however, was different. I wasn't thinking about lights, cameras or action. I was pondering only one thing: Why was John Gilman here? What was God trying to tell me?

We were in the balcony — that's where the best seats are always found. People around us were sipping Limca, a carbonated lemonade drink, and Thumbs Up, the Indian version of Coca-Cola.

The lights in the theater dimmed, and the projector flooded the screen with the production. From the beginning I kept asking my friend, "Is it biblical? Are they telling the real story?"

"Oh, it is good. It's really good," he kept assuring me.

A Second Shock

Within the first ten minutes I realized that someone had done his homework. The all-Indian cast was telling the story of the New Testament and making it come alive to people of another culture. God was going to send His only Son to earth. He was to be incarnate — born of a virgin. Then came a montage of the Lord's early life before the dramatic story unfolded.

The audience was totally absorbed. Jesus, it seemed, was more than an actor on the screen. They loved Him and identified with the Savior. This was much more than a historical drama.

Watching the life of Christ in an Indian theater was something I certainly hadn't planned. But my earlier shock at seeing the billboard was nothing compared to what happened next. I was riveted to my chair with the sudden realization: I had seen this film before!

The cinema was hot and steamy, but goose bumps ran up and down my arms as my thoughts jumped back ten years to April 1968 in Portsmouth, Virginia. It was there, in Pat Robertson's empty office at CBN, that I had an encounter with God that changed me forever. After a lifetime of resisting God's Spirit, I was overwhelmed by a power I never knew existed. Instead of praying with closed eyes, they were wide open. Before me, on an empty wall, a movie screen appeared. It was three or four feet wide.

On that "screen" I saw the life of Jesus unfold from incarnation to ascension. The scenes were in color, and I cried aloud as I watched the story of Christ. The miracles. The cross. The resurrection. There was no projector behind me, but I saw it, and it set in motion a series of events that had led me to this unlikely village.

Now, here in India, I was viewing the same story again.

This time the screen was huge, and so was the audience. I felt overcome with awe at what God was doing in John Gilman's life — like a small drop of water on the Lord's ocean of mercy.

The crowd in the theater was both noisy and interactive. They talked back to the screen and to each other. They cheered when Jesus drove the money-changers out of the temple. When He healed the blind man and the leper, they broke into applause. Other times they would laugh or sigh or cry softly.

Without question, this was a powerful and compelling production. But I wasn't prepared for what happened when Jesus was crucified on the cross. People all across the movie house began to shout, "They're killing an innocent man!" Many actually screamed for the soldiers to stop. (I found out later that movie house managers complained because the audience used up every piece of tissue paper in the theater to wipe their tears.) As the nails were driven into Jesus' hands and feet, their emotions changed from anger to sadness. Many weeped openly, shocked and despondent at what was happening to the Son of God. The soft glow from the screen allowed me to see scores of tear-stained faces.

A Great Light

This was not a gospel-hardened American audience that knew what would happen next. They had not experienced a lifetime bombardment of daily Christian radio and television. Ministers were not the subject of prime-time comedies and motion pictures. Many had never even heard of Jesus and were caught by surprise at the unfolding events.

When Christ rose from the dead, the audience whistled and clapped their hands for joy. They were wild with happiness when they saw that Jesus was alive.

What about me? I couldn't control the tears as I saw the effect of the gospel in this faraway land. My mind was racing with all kinds of thoughts. There were nearly one *billion* people in India — most of them Hindus who worship over 300 million gods. I believed this film held the answer to the hopelessness of reincarnation and the continual blood sacrifices to idols of stone.

The people in this theater were learning who God really was. They were understanding His love, His forgiveness, His grace and His great sacrifice that brings eternal life. I thought of the words of the prophet Isaiah, "The people who walked in darkness have seen a great light; those who dwelt in the land of the shadow of death, upon them a light has shined" (Is. 9:2).

When the nearly three-hour production ended with Christ's ascension, I sat paralyzed — almost dumbfounded — while the people filed out. I was drained emotionally. Finally I turned to my friend and said, "This is the most powerful tool of evangelism I have ever seen."

He agreed.

Again I was confronted with the troubling thought: What am I going to do? The film has already been made!

My ego almost prevented me from understanding what I had just witnessed. Then God said to me, "John, I have not only sent you to India, but I have prepared the way."

I looked closely at the credits on the film. The role of Jesus was portrayed by the same man who produced it — Vijay Chandar.

Who is he? Where does he live? And why did he make this film? I had many more questions than answers. The only thing I knew was that I must find Mr. Chandar as quickly as possible!

Strong and Proud

Culturally, India was light years away from where I was born in Ashland, Virginia. But in many ways life was just the same. When I was a toddler, during World War II, we moved to Newport News, where my father found work at the shipyard. Finances, however, were a continual problem.

I can still feel the embarrassment of going barefooted for lack of shoes and attending birthday parties with a hand-me-down gift. The church we attended was the one within closest walking distance since we had no car. It was about three miles away. Little did I realize that God was planting within me a deeply rooted sensitivity to the poor.

My mother, Mary Lou Beale Gilman, was a devout Christian. Arthur, my father, started attending Bible studies conducted by men at the shipyard and received Christ as his Savior. I was only about five, but old enough to see that Dad's bad habits were transformed one by one. The compassion of Jesus was shining through, and a family altar was started in our home.

I can clearly remember the Christmas morning, after my little brother, Stu, and I opened our gifts, when Dad said, "Boys, I want you to choose a couple of your presents, and we're going to give them to a family in the church that isn't having much of a Christmas." It made a profound impression.

My mother was a strong, proud woman, almost six feet tall. She was both gentle and tough and had boundless energy — at least that is how I like to remember her.

"I can't stand on my left leg!" Mom cried out to Dad early one Sunday morning. I was just a second-grader, but I knew something was terribly wrong.

When her illness first struck, about a year earlier, we

were living in the small community of Denbigh. We frequently walked together to the doctor's office. More and more often she would say, "John, let's sit here and rest a bit."

Then one day my father told Stu and me, "Your mother has rheumatoid arthritis. She may be sick a long time."

When I overheard Mom and Dad talking about what the doctors were saying, I thought, They must be talking about someone else, not Mom!

At first she hobbled around the house and tried to fix a few meals in the kitchen, but soon that stopped. It wasn't long before she became bedridden. Her knees swelled increasingly, and she became more crippled and deformed week by week.

In one year she had gone from a strong, active, energetic woman to a helpless, bedridden patient — an invalid at age forty-five.

The incomprehensible suffering my mother endured for the next fifteen years would do much more than teach me principles of eternal value. It would directly affect the lives of millions of people in the nations of the world.

It was during her illness, when I was eleven, that I attended vacation Bible school at the Denbigh Baptist Church. Mr. Phillips, who had traveled the world with the navy, told us stories of exotic lands where people had never heard the name of Jesus. It was at that moment the Lord began to deal with my heart. Then, when Pastor Bob Boyd presented the simple plan of salvation and said, "If you would like to become a Christian, please come forward," I climbed over four or five pews to accept the Lord. The walk home was nearly two miles, but it felt like two blocks.

Clinging to a Pencil

My little brother and I grew up in a hurry. We assumed increasing responsibilities as Mom's condition deteriorated. But in the process, we were still kids. We even had a good time with the wheelchair, racing it around the tiny living room as if we were at the Indianapolis 500.

Once we tried to do the wash in our rickety old washing machine with the rollers on top. But we put in so much soap powder that the suds oozed out and wouldn't stop. The floor was ankle deep in bubbles, and they began to invade the next room. We didn't know whether to laugh or cry as we rushed to carry fifty buckets of suds out the door.

Dad continued to labor at the shipyard and tend to our little crop of butterbeans, corn and potatoes — anything to save money. Our plow wasn't made for horses or even a motor. It was a "people" plow. Stu and I would pull it, and Dad would guide the plow to make the row straight.

One Saturday he caught some possum. We wanted them for pets, but they were on our plates for dinner.

For a while Mom was able to cling to a pencil — enough to write a grocery list. Eventually this simple exercise proved to be too painful. The time came when Stu and I took turns sleeping near her hospital-type bed so we could administer the medicine and empty the bedpan.

Our home was at the dead end of a dirt road called Jacobs Lane. The road ended at our house, about a quarter of a mile through the woods. It wasn't really a house, but a small cinder-block structure that had been designed to be a double garage for a house that was never built.

Mom could stare out the window to see an occasional rabbit, or a squirrel on a nearby gumball tree, but that was about all. To call us when we were outside, she used an "ooga horn" — the kind used on submarines — that Dad rigged up to a switch she could reach easily. One blast for

John, two blasts for Stu and three blasts for emergencies. We would come running from a mile away.

Deep inside I was embarrassed at our situation, never telling anyone at school my mother was an invalid. I walked the long way to the school bus so the other kids wouldn't know where I lived.

Despite our poverty, Dad saw to it that Mom received the best medical attention available. He even scraped together enough for us to have Lisi, a wonderful nurse, come to the house on weekdays to help.

For the last eight years of her life, Mom never left her room except for one final journey to the hospital. She couldn't come to my high school graduation. She couldn't sit on the front row at the wedding when I married my high school sweetheart, Caroline. We rushed home to tell her all about it.

Mom's Secret Weapon

In the long years Mother spent lying in that bed, I never heard a word of complaining. She was completely incapacitated but was the picture of peace and contentment— a testimony of God's love in the face of pain.

Mom was a living letter. In her vegetable-like condition, she couldn't go to church or hold a Bible and only rarely tried to watch television. But, oh, could she pray!

It was the dimension of prayer that gave Mom's life both purpose and productivity. She knew the reality and presence of God. Although she never said it, I know she was motivated by the fact that she could do nothing for us physically. She more than made up for it by interceding to God on our behalf. She couldn't help us, but the Lord could. Prayer was her secret weapon.

Can a weak and hurting woman play a key role in building God's eternal kingdom? Absolutely. That's how

God works. "For you see your calling, brethren, that not many wise according to the flesh, not many mighty, not many noble, are called. But God has chosen the foolish things of the world to put to shame the wise, and God has chosen the weak things of the world to put to shame the things which are mighty; and the base things of the world and the things which are despised God has chosen, and the things which are not, to bring to nothing the things that are, that no flesh should glory in His presence" (1 Cor. 1:26-29).

As the years passed, I realized that Mother's prayers were following me like the shirt on my back. She stockpiled an inheritance of intercession for me.

In November 1963 the end began. She was racked with agonizing cramps, unable to move even slightly to accommodate her body's functions. Over her objections, we moved her to a hospital where the doctors literally had to break her legs at the knees so that her calves would not continue to press against her thighs, where the flesh was decaying. The pain was unspeakable.

Finally, at barely seventy-five pounds, heavily sedated and with her gray hair thinned, she breathed a final prayer: "I thank You, Father, for seeing fit to take me home tonight."

She then hummed the words of the old familiar hymn by William J. Kirkpatrick: "I've wandered far away from God; now I'm coming home. Coming home. Coming home. Never more to roam."

At 6:20 A.M., on January 4, 1964, I stood at the foot of her bed gazing at her lifeless form beneath the sheet that covered her up to the shoulders. I rocked the bed ever so slightly, causing her feet to move left to right just a little. The Lord assured me, "She is not here. She has a new body now. This was just her house on earth." Death had transferred her to heaven.

From her bed of weakness, her prayers lit a flame of divine power that has become an intense light in a world of darkness.

The Seed Is Planted

When I was twelve, a missionary to India visited our church. He wore a sikh-like turban on his head that caught my attention. On the church bus that night I told my friends, "I'm going to be a missionary to India."

To them it must have sounded like bragging, but in that service the Holy Spirit planted a seed in my soul that would germinate and never stop growing.

The circumstances of my life left me with an inferiority complex. I felt unworthy and rejected at every turn. There were momentary flashes of optimism, but I had no expectation of being anything more than an average, ordinary person. As a result I was careless with my time and avoided much thought of purpose or aspiration.

My only natural talent seemed to be creative art and sculpture, but I wasn't motivated enough to think of it as a career.

The challenges regarding my future came from evangelists who visited our church. Their words still ring in my ears. Of the lost, they said, "Their blood will be on your hands." "God is calling you, so serve Him with all your heart, mind and soul." "You must surrender to the still, small voice of the Holy Spirit," they pleaded. But I liked the words, "Little is much when God is in it!"

While I was in high school, our youth group went to a missions conference at Calvary Baptist Church in Lancaster, Pennsylvania. It was a huge gathering. The speaker had just finished a great sermon on the words of Paul: "Therefore we are ambassadors for Christ, as though God were pleading through us: we implore you on Christ's behalf, be reconciled to God" (2 Cor. 5:20).

He asked three pointed questions: "Do you believe this verse is saying that *every* Christian is to be an ambassador for Christ?" Yes, I agreed. "If you believe that, will you circle the word 'we' in your Bible?" I did. "If you really believe that you are an ambassador, will you stand to your feet?"

I had to make an instant decision. Either I did believe it or I did not. My heart pounded as my body leaped straight up. "Yes," I said, "I believe I am an ambassador of Christ."

Then the speaker presented a more difficult challenge. "If you really, really believe God has a call to world missions on your life, and you feel the voice of the Holy Spirit saying, 'Surrender all and follow Me,' I want you to raise your hand right where you are."

It was a great leap from being a shy senior high student to announcing my ambassadorship before almost two thousand people, but that's what I was about to do. At the age of seventeen I was giving my life away. The fear and anxiety of the unknown and my feelings of inferiority almost overwhelmed me. At the same time, however, I felt an even more potent force surround me. A great confidence filled my heart — a sense of the reality of God's love for me. What could be more important than being a representative of the Savior of the world?

Immediately I stepped on my tiptoes and extended my hand as high as it would go. "Yes, Lord," I said, "I'll be Your ambassador."

It was the most powerful commitment I had ever made in my life. I was just an ordinary boy, willing to become extraordinary for the Lord. From that moment my total dependence was on Him.

If the truth were known, I went to the missions conference for only one reason: I wanted to check out the

Lancaster School of the Bible as a place to get away from home and live as I wanted to live — even if I wasn't sure what that meant.

My decision at the conference changed everything.

A Visit From Mr. Phillips

When I returned home, everyone in my family and in the church recognized my newfound zeal. They applauded me and then seemed to forget about it.

Mr. Phillips was different. He was a retired U.S. Navy captain who in middle age answered the same call to which I had responded. I had admired him since the first time I saw him at vacation Bible school when I was just eleven. To me he was a real, live missions hero — and he hadn't even made it to the field.

Just before he was to put his family on a fifty-two-foot schooner and sail to the Alaskan frontier to spend his life reaching the Eskimos, Mr. Phillips unexpectedly stopped by our little house.

He said only a few words — as if he knew too many would spoil the sacredness of what he was about to do. He reached out and took my hand, placing his palm down over mine. I felt something between our hands as he spoke. "John, I want to give you this to encourage you to keep the commitment you have made to the Lord. I want to be the first to reach out and support you. This ten dollars isn't much, but it will remind you that I am praying for you and that God has His hand on your life, son."

I was elated. My chest burst with joy and pride. He couldn't help but see the small drop of water that trickled from my eye. Mother was lying helplessly a few feet away. Her prayers had not been in vain.

"You'll never know what this means to me, Mr. Phillips."

TWO

A DREAM
TAKES SHAPE

Here's your assignment," the professor said during my freshman year in college. "Pick any nation of the world and write a research paper about it."

I chose India.

Instead of enrolling at Lancaster, my friends in Newport News encouraged me to send an application to Bob Jones University in Greenville, South Carolina. It was a fundamentalist, interdenominational college known for its literal interpretation of the Bible and commitment to evangelism. I knew their reputation for strict rules and student discipline, but deep inside I knew that was exactly what I needed at that point in my life.

Although I was now in South Carolina, my heart was back in Virginia. Yes, my mother was lying on her death-bed, but something else was tugging at me. It was a girl I had met in my ninth-grade homeroom. The first time I saw her she was wearing a little white dress, and her auburn hair was swept back gracefully. If there was ever love at first sight, this was it. Her name was Caroline Wood.

I would sit with her in the stands at the Warwick High School football games, but being so ashamed of our poverty, I never talked about my family or allowed her to visit our humble home. The closer we became, the more I tried to discourage our relationship. Finally I told her, "I'm going to have to stop seeing you because I've decided to devote myself to artwork and sculpturing." It was a flimsy excuse to keep her from learning the truth about me. It didn't work.

Later I learned that she had her father drive down our little dirt road where she could see our house through the trees. She would have him stop the car, hoping to see me. Caroline was in love too. That's all that mattered.

During my second year at Bob Jones University, she enrolled as a freshman. The following summer, in 1961, we were married.

That's All I Know

From my earliest memories it seemed I was destined to be a preacher. When I was five, Stu and I would set up a little platform in the house and play church. One day I would sing and he would preach; the next day we'd switch roles.

Mom and Dad were so proud when I brought home a copy of *Halley's Bible Handbook*. It was a prize I'd won for memorizing the most Scripture verses at vacation Bible school. And every visiting preacher at our church could count on at least one person to rededicate his life to full-time service — *me*.

Now, at college, I was searching for direction, and the pressures of life were taking their toll. I was working my way through school, deeply concerned about what was happening at home. More than once I had to drop out of college for a semester to earn the funds to continue.

After Mom's death I spent a great deal of time thinking about her desires for my life. At one point I looked up to heaven and said aloud, "Mom, don't worry. I'm going to do good."

I began keeping a little diary, and one day I felt led to write: *"I am called and I am chosen. That's all I know."*

My classmates in Greenville seemed to know exactly where they were heading, and they'd ask about my future. "Are you going to be a pastor, an evangelist, a missionary or a teacher?" To be honest, I didn't have the answer. I simply knew there was a call on my life, even if the Lord had to create a brand-new category.

When my schooling was finished at Bob Jones University, Caroline and I returned to Newport News to build a future. Our first son, John, had just been born five days before Christmas, and I had a family to support. I went to the shipyard with the idea of getting a job as a draftsman because of my drawing skills. It was a huge department, with over two hundred employees.

"I don't understand it," said the foreman who was interviewing me. "You've studied for the ministry, and now you want to be a draftsman?"

I didn't understand it either.

"Well, sir," I told him, "I just want to pay my bills and be a good Christian." Then I added, "If you'll hire me and give me a chance to learn, I'll take some courses and be the best draftsman you have."

He hired me! Four days later I was to report for work to begin a long-term commitment to secular work. Was I about to forget the promise I made to God at the Lancaster missionary conference? Did Mr. Phillips make a bad investment when he gave me that ten dollars?

I justified my decision by thinking, I can do some part-time ministry — perhaps some child evangelism.

The Lord, however, often works in strange and unobtrusive ways. Flashing through my mind were seven words my mother-in-law added as a footnote in a letter to Caroline. We received it just before leaving Greenville. Mrs. Wood had written, "WXRI is looking for cameramen and announcers."

Those call letters rang a bell. It was a Christian radio station in Portsmouth, about a thirty-minute drive across the James River from Newport News. The station had been started by a man named Pat Robertson under the umbrella of the Christian Broadcasting Network. It really wasn't a network, just a small, low-powered radio station.

I couldn't figure out why a radio station would be advertising for cameramen, but radio interested me. I thought, With my new full-time job, it would be great if they'd let me produce a children's program every weekend.

When I arrived at WXRI, there wasn't much to see. It was in a dilapidated building on Spratley Street built beside a garbage dump in an older section of town. There was a little UHF television station there too. I parked on the muddy lot and tried to find someone who knew about the openings they had advertised.

Robertson, the man behind this fledgling ministry, was out of town, but they introduced me to Jay Arlan and Bill Garthwaite. Arlan was head of the radio station. To my surprise, they interviewed me all day. They also offered me a full-time job with two titles: art director and audio engineer. Starting pay, $1.25 an hour.

Logically, there was no question of what I should do. Employment at the shipyard offered much higher pay, benefits for my family and the promise of a great future. My heart, however, was telling me something altogether different.

"Caroline, what should I do?"

"Honey," she said, "this is the Lord's leading. I feel you should join CBN. God will take care of us."

The drafting job in Newport News was shipwrecked. Again Mother's prayers were being answered.

Zippy the Mailbox

The titles I was given at CBN were misleading. I designed creative graphics and ran the audio board, but there was much more to be done. The budget was tight, the staff was small, and the task was enormous. One hour I'd be hosting a program, the next I'd be cleaning commodes. On the nightly children's program I was everything from Zippy the Mailbox to the director of the show. The lack of funds didn't faze us since we were caught up in a great vision.

Caroline and I were involved in a local Baptist church. One day the pastor said, "John, I believe it's time for you to commit yourself to full-time ministry. I'd like you to become our associate pastor."

I'd been at CBN a year and a half and thought I *was* involved in ministry, but I agreed to pray about his offer. It seemed the right thing to do. For the next year I served the church, but I was like a nomad in the desert. Never was I so thirsty for the things of God. Even as a Christian I was battling with a deep inner feeling that my heart was desperately wicked. I was falling short of His glory and felt so unworthy of what Christ had done for me.

Day after day I prayed, "Lord, show me Your divine direction for my life. Cleanse me, use me, God. Shower me with a baptism of Your love."

Every time I opened the New Testament and read the accounts of the disciples' dynamic faith, I'd ask, Shouldn't that be happening now? I had studied the lives of great men of God such as Moody, Finney and Spurgeon. "Lord, I must have more of You," I prayed. "I want to glorify Your name."

At night I'd flip the television dial to see what was happening back at CBN. Deep inside I wished I had never left. One evening John Osteen, a Baptist pastor from Texas, was a guest on "The 700 Club." When he talked about the miracles that were happening in his ministry, I was deeply stirred with a longing to surrender all.

The next day I drove over to CBN to deliver the tapes of our church radio program to WXRI. It was in April 1968. During my visit I walked into the TV control room while they were finishing the taping of a program that was to air that night. Again Robertson was interviewing John Osteen.

After the program Osteen and Robertson walked back into the control room. Pat introduced John to me, and I said nervously, "Last night I was watching you on television, and when you showed that boy in India who was healed of club feet, I began to weep. I said, 'This is the Jesus I have been looking for.' "

Osteen said, "John, I've never met anyone so ready to receive what God has for him. Will you let me pray with you?"

I nodded in agreement.

"Where can we go?" Osteen asked.

"You can use my new office," said Robertson.

We walked up the steps to an office so new that Pat had

yet to move in. There was no carpet. The cinder-block walls were painted white, and the pictures hadn't been hung. There was a beautiful cherry wood desk with a new olive green executive chair behind it.

Osteen invited me to sit in the big chair, and he said, "Let's worship the Lord together."

At that moment I released my entire being to the Lord; it was like nothing I had ever experienced. I didn't know when the Texas pastor left the room, and I didn't care.

Like another John, "I was in the Spirit on the Lord's Day" (Rev. 1:10). I "baptized" Pat's new desk with tears of joy. At least it was sprinkled.

One Grain of Sand

It was at that moment that I saw the screen appear on the freshly painted wall and a "movie" of the life of Christ flash before me. The scenes about Jesus made me want to praise Him even more. When the crucifixion appeared, the Spirit said to me, "Don't be afraid. Only I would show you this." Then He said, "You're seeing only one grain of sand of My holiness in a mighty ocean."

After about twenty minutes I said, "Lord, what do I do next?" He said, "Go into the next room and love your brother." In the next office was a Methodist preacher. We hugged like long lost cousins.

That day I became a transformed person, and I didn't care who knew it. My inferiority complex was gone — forever. It seemed like a river bubbling inside me. I could not stop thinking of His glory and praise. I was truly filled with His love. For a conservative, independent Baptist, that was something.

Within a few days I resigned my position with the church and was back at CBN. Before long I was production manager, in charge of network programming, and a regular host on "The 700 Club."

One day a man from India appeared in my office. His name was Mark Ivan. He shared with me the burden of his country. He was finishing his education in America and was anxious to return to his wife and children, whom he hadn't seen in five years.

It seemed I couldn't stop asking questions about his country. He handed me a copy of a dissertation he wrote at Howard University. The title shocked me: "Two Thousand Years of the Holy Spirit in India." It was true. The apostle Thomas ("Doubting" Thomas) was martyred in Madras, according to popular tradition. This foreign missionary idea wasn't so new after all.

With increasing frequency my thoughts turned to fulfilling the Great Commission. If we could use modern communication strategies to reach Norfolk and the United States, why not the villages and hamlets of the entire world?

Heading for Haiti

It was just a small book, but I couldn't throw it away. The title was *Little David Walker*.

I was in an empty Studio B at CBN cleaning out boxes and throwing out the trash when I spotted the small volume. I remembered hearing "Little David" on the radio when I was about nine years old. The boy preacher was about my age.

I wondered whatever became of him, as I leafed through the book. That evening I read it from cover to cover. I wanted to meet this man and talk with him about the power of God in his ministry.

Exactly two days later Little David — he wasn't so little now — walked into the studio. I met him and said, "You'll never believe this, but I just finished reading a book about you!"

"Let's go to lunch and talk about it," he said.

I phoned Caroline, and we went to the Holiday Inn in Portsmouth. Before the meal had finished I was pouring out my heart to him concerning my deep burden for world evangelism.

"Why don't you go to Haiti with us?" he said.

"That sounds exciting!" I responded. "We'll pray about it and call you as soon as possible."

At that time we were trying to buy a small home and were faced with a real choice. It was either put a down payment on the home or buy two round-trip tickets to Haiti. We couldn't do both. After seeking the Lord, we decided to put our faith on the line. During the Christmas break we flew to Port au Prince to help David Walker with a missions project.

While we were there I felt compelled to find a movie house. I wanted to see how people in another land responded to the medium of film.

The cinema was nothing more than four walls with no ceiling. The place was packed with two thousand Haitians who had paid less than ten cents to watch a James Bond-type movie. I climbed up to the projection room to get a better view.

What covered the silver screen broke my heart. Under that canopy of stars, I was repulsed by what "Christian" America had exported to these people. It was garbage — worse than the squalor and poverty of their daily lives. Here were some of the poorest people of the world who had scraped together a few pennies for a night of entertainment, but the gratuitous violence and sex that flooded the screen was a product of my own country. I was angry and ashamed.

My heart was full as I looked out over the audience through one of the unused projection windows and prayed, "Lord, it isn't right that these precious people should have to pay for this filth while the greatest nation on earth does not share the gospel with them." Then I said, "By Your grace, I vow to come to this theater someday and fill that screen with the message of Jesus and His love."

That prayer set my soul on fire. The flame was small, but it warmed my spirit. I became totally committed to using the creative imagination God had given me for only one purpose — to reach the lost.

I knew the rest of my life would be wrapped up in the vow I made beside that grinding 35mm motion picture projector in the darkness of that dingy Haitian movie house. At that moment, in the winter of 1970, I determined to do something about "visualizing" the gospel in the culture of the local people. That was more important than any home I could ever purchase.

My unquenchable appetite for world evangelism became even greater after being asked by CBN to handle television production for the Nora Lam crusade in Taiwan.

One night six thousand people crowded our platform and almost tore it down in their desire to receive the Lord and be prayed for. That scene has never left my memory. At one point I was desperately trying to keep a large television light pole from falling over on the mass of humanity beneath me. I was almost overcome by the body heat of the crowd in the stifling, humid air.

I can still see women with perspiration streaming down their faces — beneath them were little babies who were beginning to suffocate. The eyes of those who came were hurting and empty. Their hands reached out as they cried for the Savior.

More than a hundred thousand people attended the crusades that were watched by an estimated TV audience of twelve million Chinese. There had never been such a response to the gospel on that island.

Wrestling With Questions

From my office at CBN I could look down into Studio B where "The 700 Club" set stood. Behind me was a monitor that allowed me to watch various television productions in progress.

One particular day I was contemplating how I should be involved in spreading the gospel. I was also thinking about CBN's role. My experiences in Haiti and Taiwan were permanently etched on my mind.

I thought, You are the director of programming for the world's only Christian television network. Do you know what to do? Do you know how to reach thirty-six million children who have never gone to Sunday school or church in America? What about the inner-city youth? Do you have any concept for reaching black and Hispanic America? Are you so deeply entrenched in a white, middle-class mentality that you'll never know how to help your brothers of other ethnic cultures?

The questions would not stop coming: Just because you have a vast TV network that broadcasts to a huge potential audience, can you produce any programs that will penetrate the unreached in North America, such as the Jewish community? What about the millions of Arabs and Chinese and Koreans and Indians living here? Can you reach them? What about the emotionally disturbed who number in the tens of millions? How about chemical abusers in the drug culture?

As I thought about the challenge of being given twenty-four hours a day for programming, my mind was flooded with questions and my heart ached to know the answers. Will God not hold us accountable for what we produce? Were we to continue simply to preach the gospel via "talking head" shows and the conventional forms of communicating, or could we enter the arena of creativity and innovation?

For more than an hour I had been sitting at my desk, staring out that large viewing window. In the past the most powerful means of evangelism had been preaching and teaching from a platform. Paul and Peter did it. Moody did it. Billy Graham did it, and we were now doing it effectively on television.

Would it be wrong to act out the Bible stories in a culturally relevant manner? Of course, drama had been used in ministry over the years. Plays, movies and mime had all been effective. But now I was rethinking the whole process for the nation's first Christian broadcasting network.

Then I thought, Where does the Spirit of God fit into all of this? Should we go on TV with total dependence on the Spirit's inspiration, or should we plan every production down to the millisecond?

Other questions bombarded my mind. What about pre-evangelism? Should we produce programs which include worldliness — and espouse principles to which we are opposed — in order to portray a moral theme subtly? Is it valid to produce *The Godfather: Part V* so we can have someone read from Scripture at a gangster's grave? Should Christians invest millions to produce a pop-music special so they can slip in a non-offensive gospel song?

The last thought I had that day was perhaps the most perplexing. Why was it that the art of communicating the gospel was not as perfected as the art of communicating in general? Why? I laid my head in my arms on the desk and began to pray. "O God, show me what to do."

For me, wrestling with these questions was agony. I

truly felt a sense of destiny as I pleaded, "Lord, I have to know Your answer. I don't want to stand before You having helped lead this network down the wrong path."

You Do the Same

Then the answer came. It was not an audible voice, but very clearly I heard instructions that would later touch the lives of millions. The Lord said, "I want you to do the same thing I did when I was on earth. I spoke to the people in parables and stories. You do the same."

There it was. So simple. So real. I wiped my anguished face on my shirt sleeve and breathed a deep sigh. God had spoken to me, and I knew it.

Now I started to imagine the millions of unreached living in the villages and hamlets of Africa, India, China and South America. I had done this before, but now I put myself in their mud huts. I felt their frustration over not knowing the truth about the great Creator God except through the devilish eyes of the local witch doctor, temple priest or ancestor-worshipping grandfather. I became ecstatic over the possibilities of going into that village and presenting the answer. My mind began to whirl.

First I thought of all the means Christian missionaries and evangelists had used thus far to penetrate the darkness of minds and hearts. A friend of mine in college had sold everything and brought his wife and family of seven children to Greenville while he studied for a lifetime of service on the mission field. The last day I saw Jim, we prayed together. He owned no watch, so I slipped mine off and handed it to him. I wondered how he could be so brave to pack his barrels of belongings and head for another two years in a French-language school getting ready to enter the field of his calling — the nation of Niger in Africa.

He committed his family to a lifetime of living the Christian witness before absolute foreigners. How could he face the scorching summer nights, the disease, the new culture and the absence of fellowship for his family?

How long would it be before one convert would be his? Would he become terminally ill and die before his mission was done? I had only the highest admiration for Jim but was starting to question our traditional methods of reaching the world.

Which Way to Go?

Who was I to criticize? Hadn't Americans like Billy Graham and T.L. Osborn brought hundreds of thousands to Christ in foreign cultures preaching through native interpreters? But who was doing the follow-up?

What about the billions of gospel tracts that have been given to people who can't even read? Is the "one soul is worth the whole world" strategy justified regardless of the cost?

And what about radio? Christian shortwave stations have beamed the message for years — yet most people we need to reach have never seen a receiver.

Then I dwelt on the possibilities of television, a profession I was mastering. As I looked into just how many people in the world received a television signal, I was amazed to realize that it would be decades before half the world ever had the possibility of watching a program. In India alone more than half a billion had never seen a TV set. Worldwide there were fewer than 400 million TV sets [in 1973], and most of those were in Europe and North America.

Is it any longer right to export a Western presentation of Jesus? Why would Africans or Chinese care to see or hear the almost totally white Anglo-Saxon Protestant portrayal of the greatest story ever told? Is there a more excellent way?

I listed the advantages and disadvantages of every known method of evangelism. There was no question in my mind that the gospel story on film, produced in the language and culture of the people, would be the most powerful tool of evangelism — and the most cost-effective — since the Lord challenged us with the Great Commission.

I couldn't wait to share it with Pat Robertson and the executives at CBN. Without question, they would immediately establish an international film division.

I couldn't wait!

THREE

RISKING IT ALL

My excitement for reaching the world through film consumed me. Every day at CBN I prayed, "Lord, what do I do?" The concept God gave me in Haiti grew until I felt ready to explode.

I wondered, How many Chinese are there? How many in India? What about Africa? How could we reach them? What if we filmed the story of Christ with all native actors? What if we had mobile film units to show it free in every village? What if? What if?

For months I had planted the seeds of my vision to the executives at CBN. Now I was becoming bold in my proposal that we set up an entire ministry division for film evangelism. At every executive meeting I'd look for the right moment to touch on the topic.

Then one day after I broached the subject in an important meeting with my colleagues, Pat Robertson turned to me like a father lecturing his son and said, "Brother, quit talking about film."

I got the message.

That night I fell to my knees and cried out for an answer. The Lord whispered: "John, I haven't given this vision to Pat; I've given it to *you*!"

The Little Book

It was a bright spring Saturday afternoon in Portsmouth. The weeds in my backyard were starting to grow, and I knew it was time to do a little gardening.

"Come over here, John. I've got something I'd like to give you." It was the voice of my next-door neighbor, a retired Methodist minister who lived alone. He leaned over the fence that separated our yards, and I noticed he had a small book in his hand.

"Thank you very much," I said as he presented the volume of about 120 pages.

He was a warm, friendly man, but I didn't hold him in very high esteem as a minister. Once I attended a church where he spoke and felt his sermon was a social message with little spiritual content. To be honest, I was rather judgmental in those days and even wondered if he was really a Christian.

On a previous afternoon we had been chatting, and he invited me into his home. We walked into his study, and I was immediately curious about the books on his shelves. To my disappointment, there were only a few meager volumes. I thought, I'm thirty years younger and have a library twenty times that size. I felt justified in my thoughts of his spiritual condition.

On this afternoon I didn't even glance at the book's contents because I was so sure that anything he gave me would be of very little value or substance. I walked into the house and placed it in one of my bookcases.

This was a pivotal period in my life. I was obsessed with a passion to reach the lost. Two specific burdens continued to weigh on me heavily: the people of India and film evangelism. I saw an endless sea of people without the Savior, and I saw a method by which they could be saved. Every time I closed my eyes to pray, these two themes were the focus of my thoughts. But just how were these burdens going to mix?

There was one thing I *did* realize. I knew that if the dream God placed within my heart was to be fulfilled, I couldn't look to others to see it accomplished. Ultimately, as the words of an old song say, it was going to be "Jesus and me."

This was a time of intense soul-searching. It seemed that God aimed His most powerful beam of light directly into my heart. He saw every weakness, every flaw and imperfection. I thought again about the words Christ had spoken during the Sermon on the Mount: "Blessed are the pure in heart: for they shall see God" (Matt. 5:8, KJV).

Seeking for more substance to fill my great hunger to know God, I studied the subject of fasting and prayer. For the first time I realized its enormous potential for spiritual development. Previously I had fasted short periods of time — a half a day here and there and sometimes an entire day. I thought about some of the great men and women of God who had committed themselves to longer periods of fasting and was convinced I needed to do the same. But that convincing came in an unusual way.

On the Spot

One night, yearning for a greater revelation of God's presence, I prayed, "Lord, You've got to speak to me. I must understand You more. I'm not satisfied with where I am, and I need Your clear direction for my life."

Suddenly I felt inspired to get out of my chair and walk over to where my books lined the walls. I began to speak out loud and couldn't believe the words I spoke. "Lord, I'm going to run my finger down this row of books and stop at a particular one. I don't know which volume, but I'm going to believe that You'll guide me and that the answer I need tonight will be in that book."

I challenged the Lord further, saying, "If I pick up the book and don't find the answer, I'll know that You really are not leading me at all — it's just my own desire." It was like a "fleece" for God's guidance.

My heart pounded as I realized I had put myself in quite a spot. Perhaps I was being too presumptuous to think that God would respond to such a bold request. Immediately I ran my fingers down the spines of a row of books. I stopped at a volume without noticing what it was. I pulled it out and was disappointed to find it was none other than the little publication the Methodist minister had handed me across the fence.

The commitment had been made, so I sat down in my well-worn easy chair and looked at the cover to see what God had in store. The title of the book was *With Christ in the School of Prayer*. It was by the missionary statesman Andrew Murray.

Reading no more than three pages, I was gripped with the fact that this was no ordinary book. I was going to be taught things for which my heart had yearned. This was going to become a holy journey, and I knew I must "set myself aside" in the process. I committed to enter a long period of fasting so as to absorb everything God wanted me to know.

A New Dimension

For the next twenty days I took no food into my body — only liquids. I continued to perform my duties at CBN and to be a husband and father to my family, but every other moment was spent in prayer and in the reading — and rereading — of this unusual book.

What I discovered in Andrew Murray's volume stunned me. I never knew there was such a dimension of prayer — actually a "school" of prayer that Jesus taught and wanted every one of His disciples to enjoy. I began to understand how His will could be accomplished and His kingdom built. The little book fit perfectly in my pocket. Every spare moment I'd read another few sentences or even an entire page.

I learned that God wanted me to have a pure heart through yielding to His Spirit. I read, I prayed and I cried. "Lord, I want to know You. I want to *see* You."

The more I read, the more I seemed to enter into the heart of God. I accepted the challenge of being with Christ in the school of prayer. Underlining passages on every page of the book, I soon nearly wore the volume to shreds from constant use. Seeking God for an absolutely pure heart in every area of my life became paramount.

During that time of fasting, praying and reading I discovered that impurities such as my judgmental spirit were keeping me from some of God's greatest blessings. So often His riches come disguised in a humble earthen vessel such as this Methodist minister whom I judged not fit to be heard.

Since then I have bought dozens of copies of this life-changing book and given them to friends who longed to see Jesus in a new and greater dimension.

Before the Lord could use me, He had to *change* me. Now I felt I was ready.

"It's Driving Me Nuts"

From 1976 to 1978 I had wrestled enough to join Hulk Hogan on national television. The struggle, however, wasn't against flesh and blood but was instead an internal battle that often left me fatigued and exhausted. Day after day I debated about leaving CBN even though the vision of Christian television pulsated through my being. In the natural, it would be a horrendous mistake. The network was ready to move from its tiny facilities at Portsmouth to modern headquarters in Virginia Beach, and my career as a broadcast professional was at its zenith.

Once, during that time of decision, I sat in the front seat of a car with Robertson and said, "Pat, this is hard for me to say, but I can't get this burden to reach the world through film out of my heart — it's driving me nuts. It is not a question of loyalty. I'd literally give my life for you and this ministry, but I don't know what to do." Then I added, "Would you pray that God would lift this burden?"

"If that's what you want me to do, I'll pray," said Pat compassionately.

The burden didn't lift; in fact, it became heavier. The idea of mobile film units going from village to village was more than a dream. It was so clear it seemed tangible. And it was more than just India. I saw the same thing happening in Africa, China and Latin America.

No electricity? I thought. That's not a problem. We'll bring a portable generator. We don't even need a screen — just a bedsheet hanging between two trees. I could see it all.

Finally, on a spring night in April 1978, I sat down and

wrote the rationale of why the vision would never be fulfilled by staying at CBN. The next morning, on the way to the office, I turned on my little micro-cassette and began to dictate, "Dear Pat: This is the most difficult letter I have ever written." The last words on the tape were: "I am going to go to India."

I dictated my resignation with firm conviction, yet with fear and trepidation. Without question it was the biggest step of faith I had ever taken. I parked the car, took my little recorder and headed for the office.

The phone rang the minute I sat down at my desk. "Hello, John," the voice on the line said. "This is John Gimenez." He was pastor of a large church in Virginia Beach.

"I'm having dinner tomorrow with a group of people from India. They're fixing a special Indian meal. Would you like to come?"

My heart almost stopped beating. "Would I? John, don't say anything. I want you to hear the last words I just dictated."

I grabbed my recorder, tapped the reverse button and played back the last sentence: "I'm going to go to India."

"I'll be there," I told him.

The Lamb Who Was a Lion

On Saturday Caroline and I went to the small home of some Indian Christians. About fifteen people packed the dining room.

At the dinner was a little fellow about five-foot-three wearing a slightly tattered navy blue suit. His name was Ernest Komanapalli from the state of Andhra Pradesh in South India. He seemed as gentle and quiet as a lamb.

I soon found out that looks were deceiving. In India he is a lion — a powerful giant for the Lord. Friends around the table shared the fact that this humble man had an earned doctorate and was responsible for ten orphanages, two hospitals, a Bible college and over three hundred churches. The young people he was training would become administrators of large ministries later in their lives.

Ernest was one of six boys raised in India's poverty by a Christian mother who prayed for fifty years for a spiritual awakening in India. All six of her sons entered the ministry, and now he was visiting America in an attempt to secure finances for his under-funded outreach.

When I heard his story, I broke into tears of gratitude. An inner conviction told me the Lord had sent this man to give me direction regarding my call to the land of his birth.

After the spicy Indian meal, pastor Gimenez said, "John, tell Ernest your idea for reaching the people of India."

With fear that Ernest might reject it, I shared my concept of producing a motion picture of the life of Christ with an all-Indian cast and taking it to the villages of his country.

"Yes, brother, it will work." I could see the gleam in his eyes and knew he was telling me the truth. He said, "I have already shown an old black-and-white film, *The Greatest Story Ever Told* [the 1923 Cecil B. DeMille original silent film]. It didn't have a soundtrack, so I held the microphone and gave the narration as the pictures filled the screen."

"What happened?" I interrupted.

"Brother, people got saved!"

That was all I needed to know.

A few days later, after a church service, I turned around and there was Ernest, standing about ten feet from me. When I looked at him, suddenly it seemed I saw all of India in his face. I rushed over and put my arms around him. I could not stop sobbing. He cried too as the Lord bonded our hearts together.

"What do you need?" I asked him. "How can I help you?" As we talked he told me that he'd found a man in Bombay who was going to make a little video to tell the story of his ministry. God spoke to me and said, "You make this documentary for Ernest, and I'll bless you!" It was almost a command.

For me it was such an unlikely commitment that I hesitated to tell him what I felt. My faith-talk to friends at CBN was on such a huge scale: "Well, I'm in contact with some people in Hollywood, and we're going to produce a big film on the life of Christ for India." Yes, I had talked to some people on the West Coast, and, yes, they thought it was a great idea. But where was I going to find the millions of dollars for a production budget?

Now God was telling me, "Make this little promotional film and produce it yourself." In other words, "Get your hands dirty! Show Me where your heart is. *Trust Me*."

"Ernest," I said, "I want to help you make this film, and I'll do it at my own expense."

With my own money? I had just resigned from a salaried job. In a few days I would be receiving no income at all. I had just become a missionary and was already giving away something I didn't even have!

By this time our personal responsibilities had grown. We had two wonderful sons, John Jr., age twelve, and Stephen, who was ten. Caroline worked part-time, but the financial needs of beginning an international ministry were something we could not comprehend. We knew it would take a miracle.

We placed a For Sale sign in the front yard of our home. The funds from the equity in the home, plus the few dollars we had managed to save would surely be enough to get me to India, produce the video for Ernest and keep food on the table for a little while.

A Fragmented Society

My first day in India was like looking through a kaleidoscope. It was November 1978. India at last, I thought as the humid air of Bombay's International Airport welcomed me to this amazing three-thousand-year-old culture. At every turn there was a new scene of fascinating color and variety that I'd never known before.

Here were nearly one billion people packed into a country one-third the size of the United States. It stretched from the lofty Himalayas across the broad Ganga plain to the shores of the vast Indian Ocean.

India is a union of twenty-two states and seven territories that is held together more by its diversity than its common threads. It is called the "world's largest democracy," and rightly so. The country is divided into a million self-contained and socially isolated fragments.

The fifteen official languages recognized by the constitution do not begin to tell the story. Even Hindi, the most widely used language, is not spoken by a majority. English is the only language used in every part of the country, but only three in every one hundred people speak it. Several hundred separate languages and dialects are spoken across the nation. Because of England's eighteenth-century colonization of India, several native words have come into our language, such as "bungalow," "pajama" and "calico."

The ministry of Ernest Komanapalli had its headquarters in Amalapurnam, on India's eastern coast. The impact he was making in that Telugu-speaking area was far greater than what had been described by his friends in Virginia. We met with his video producer and immediately went to work on the low-budget production.

While we worked on the project, I had no idea what the future held for Ernest — or for me.

At the time, however, I needed to know much more than what was happening in one man's ministry. I spent every available moment visiting motion picture houses to "learn the system" and find out what people responded to. It was ironic that God called me to a film ministry, and I had never produced one in my life. All of my previous media work had been in the field of video, and there is a great difference.

Plots and Subplots

Indian films are in a class all of their own. They are so far removed from reality that I had great difficulty trying to understand them. Nearly all are morality tales that uphold traditional virtues such as the goodness of poverty or the importance of chastity. Producers solve the entertainment problem by concentrating on the exact opposite of these values. For example, they usually feature characters of ostentatious wealth or ones who frequent a vulgar cabaret. Since it's the disadvantaged who make up nearly all of India's vast population, they leave the theater happy when a typical film ends with the poor rising up to defeat the rich.

The films have plots and subplots and are rather long by American standards — about two and a half hours. What amazed me was that *all* the films had several songs and dances.

I prayed, "Lord, somehow, some way, let the gospel come to these screens."

When it was time to return from my short trip, I was scratching my head about how to translate the life of Christ into a culture that was totally foreign to me. How much money would it really cost? Who could write a script that would communicate the real gospel? Where could I find competent Indian actors who would accurately portray the Christian message?

Was the concept of my own imagination, or did God really tell me to do it? It was much easier to dream about it in Virginia Beach than to come face-to-face with reality in cities like Bombay and Calcutta. I even wondered how many years it would take to see the vision come to pass.

I returned to Caroline and the boys with great questions but an even greater burden to reach this desperate nation. Week by week, finances — the lack of them — became a more serious problem. I knew, however, that I had made a commitment to Komanapalli to return and finish his video. Three months later, in February 1979, I scraped together the funds to make the journey.

That's when I saw the billboard that changed my life. For a man who was almost drowning in a God-given dream, there it was: *Daya Sagar* (Oceans of Mercy).

Seeing the gospel on the screen that night almost took my breath away. I walked out of the theater absolutely convinced that what I had just witnessed was more than an ordinary film. It was God at work. I prayed, "Lord, You revealed it to me on the wall of Pat's office. You revealed it again tonight. Now, Lord, complete the vision."

I wanted that film — not just the idea, but the very film — to be shown to every person in every village of this vast land. I could see millions upon millions spending eternity in heaven because of the Lord's mercy.

The Great Challenge

If any means of evangelism could penetrate the Hindu system of belief, this was it. Hinduism is a complex world of tradition that presents a great challenge to any representative of Christ. The caste system is divided into between two hundred and three hundred *jati* (the Indian word for "caste").

The Hindu system ranks people from polluted to pure. Only through cycles of earthly perfection and reincarnation can they hope to reach the highest rung on the ladder. The rules of caste attempt to govern such things as exchanges of food, the occupations of individuals, even restricting marriages to those within a particular group. Tradition dominates the society. Even the most urbanized families will forbid their daughters to be wed in anything other than a red sari — an attire mentioned in seventh-century Tamil texts.

Hinduism has been described as "a museum of religions." It is the world's only major faith that hasn't been traced to a specific founder and the only one that does not have a sacred book as the one and only scriptural authority. Hindus can regard the *Rig Veda* as their personal bible, or turn to the *Upanishads*, or the *Bhagavad Gita* — or read none of them and still claim to be good Hindus. They have millions of gods to choose from — or they may meditate on a "supreme spirit" that dwells somewhere inside them. It seems to make little difference whether they visit a temple or bathe in a holy river since they believe that "many paths lead to the same goal."

The country is filled with religious variety. You often see the *sadhus*, or eternal wanderers, dressed in their yellow or ocher robes — their bodies smeared with ash and their foreheads anointed with sandal-paste.

The Jains believe that nonviolence is the supreme religion. Some Jaina monks carry their beliefs to such extremes that they are often seen with their noses and mouths covered with a fine cloth so they will not unknowingly "kill" germs while breathing.

Despite decades of modernization and the influence of

Western thought, little seems to have changed. The "untouchables" were renamed by Mahatma Gandhi as "the people of God," but that has not significantly altered the way they are treated.

Even though India was a British colony for nearly a hundred years, only 3 percent of the nation is Christian.

For ten years I prayed for God to reveal a strategy to reach India — and eventually the world — for Christ, and that night I saw it. Why should only 3 percent know the Savior? Why not 30 percent? Why not 60? Why not...?

But first things first. Who was this actor-producer named Vijay [pronounced vee-jay] Chandar? Why did he produce a film about the life of Christ? Where could I find him? I was determined to locate the man as quickly as possible. Nothing seemed more important.

FOUR

THE STONE
CRIES OUT

"How can I find the producer of *Daya Sagar*?" I asked my Indian friends. "It's urgent that I meet him immediately."

We drove to the offices of film distributors inquiring, "Where can I find Vijay Chandar?" After a week of asking we were given a phone number for his production company. He lived in Madras, a major city in the state of Tamil Nadu, on India's southeast coast.

When he came to the phone I said, "This is John Gilman from the United States. I have seen your movie, and I like it very much. May I talk with you about it? Can we meet somewhere? It's very important to me."

I was encouraged by the enthusiasm in his voice as he responded, "Let's meet at the Madras airport." I purchased a ticket and rushed to meet him.

I couldn't wait to learn how he had managed to produce such an authentic account of the life of Christ. How had he achieved such a remarkable distribution of this film in the Hindu theater system?

Mr. Chandar was not hard to pick out of the crowd. He was about six-foot-two and was smartly dressed in a Nehru-style white suit. He had black hair down to his shoulders, much as he wore when he played the role of Jesus. His eyes were brown and steely. I had seen him on the screen, but he was much more impressive in person.

Later I learned that Vijay was one of India's top producers and actors, best known for playing movie "tough guys."

"I Could Not Escape It"

The chauffeur of his India-made Matador car drove us to the restaurant of a local hotel. I was anxious to know everything possible about this Hindu filmmaker. The moment we were seated at the table I began asking questions about *Oceans of Mercy*.

For more than five years he had worked on the film. The group that started the project soon ran out of money, and the production faced total cancellation. Chandar, determined to complete the movie, found new financing, picked up the pieces and continued.

"Vijay, why did you make that film?" I asked. His answer surprised me.

"Jesus made me do it" was his reply. "Something would not let the project die. I could not escape from it. The hand of God was steering my every move."

A Hindu all of his life, he was of the Brahman caste, the highest rung of their spiritual ladder. "I believed that Jesus was a good teacher but nothing more. When the opportunity to make a movie on the life of Christ came to me, I was drawn to it by an inner compulsion I did not understand," he said.

It was in 1973, five years before the production was released, that Vijay sensed God compelling him to make the film. That was the same year the Lord confirmed my own eventual direction toward India which five years later resulted in my resignation from CBN.

He told me, "The project had many problems, but I could not stop the production. It was as if God were making the film and I had no choice."

I looked directly into those steely eyes and said, "I have no choice either in what I am about to say. Jesus is compelling me to tell you to give me this motion picture. I want to take it to every village in India."

It was then I knew exactly why I had left a great ministry, sold my home, risked my future and come halfway around the world. I didn't care about the rights; I wanted the film for evangelism. What I was thinking was, Please don't prohibit me from taking this movie everywhere, because one way or another, by the grace of God, I'm going to do it. Deep inside I knew I had a divine appointment with this man that was predetermined many years before. I was commissioned!

His response was "No problem! We can work this out." I had no idea of the difficulties that would lie ahead, but at that moment I knew I was *not* going to produce this movie. It had already been done to perfection, and God's vision was about to be fulfilled.

I told him, "As surely as God has chosen you to produce this major motion picture of the life of Christ, God has chosen me to see that this film is presented in every village and hamlet in India — even if it is out in an open field with a portable projector."

To my amazement, Vijay agreed: "John, I believe that your Christ has sent you here for just that purpose." He did not realize at that moment how important that truth would become in his life.

The White Man's God?

Vijay was having great success getting his film shown in movie houses, but he did not have the vision for saturating the nation. That was to be my role. Only about 20 percent of India's population lives in the big cities. The remaining 80 percent lives in over a half-million villages where there are few theaters. By traditional methods they would never be given a chance to encounter what millions were experiencing in the darkened theaters of the cities. By Indian standards Vijay's movie was a strong box-office attraction and a commercial success.

He gave me permission to begin using the film immediately with the understanding that we would negotiate later regarding the long-term rights.

Oceans of Mercy was produced with an all-Indian cast and initially released in the Telugu language. For biblical accuracy, he sought the advice of a Christian theologian.

By the time we first met, over five million people had already heard the gospel through this dramatic film. The production breaks down all cultural barriers. Jesus is not presented as the "white man's God"; He is Indian. If He were to walk out of Nazareth into a typical village in India, He would be one of them — looking as they look, wearing similar clothing, drawing water from a well, walking the dusty roads as they do today. Almost everything would be the same. The one "who had no place to lay His head" would be loved by India's masses. If any film was on target for evangelism, this was it.

Later that night, in the privacy of my room, I fell to my knees and prayed, "Lord, I thank You for the miracle You have done today. But now I pray for Vijay. You have guided his steps and caused him to produce a motion picture that will bring millions to the kingdom. He knows *about* You, but I want him to know You personally. Amen."

A new day for missions had dawned. This is not to say that God was now bypassing the foreign missionaries and Indian evangelists who had witnessed so faithfully for several hundred years. It simply meant that God is not limited to our traditional methods.

I've been asked, "Why would a non-Christian producer from India make a film of the life of Jesus?" Perhaps the question should be, Why wouldn't an American or European do it? God will accomplish His task, even through a Hindu filmmaker.

When the disciples began to praise the Lord with a loud voice for all they had seen, the Pharisees said to Jesus, "Master, rebuke thy disciples." Jesus answered, "I tell you that, if these should hold their peace, the stones would immediately cry out" (Luke 19:39,40, KJV).

Vijay was one of God's stones.

Pieces of the Puzzle

"We've got it! We've got it!" I shouted when I told Ernest Komanapalli the great news.

Without delay we began intensive planning sessions on how to reach the 567,000 villages of India with the gospel. Our strategy was to use mobile film teams in rural areas and at the same time intensify efforts to continue showing it in the cities. Each team would consist of four people, a van, a movie projector, a screen, a portable generator, a loudspeaker and a copy of the film.

The van would drive through the village the day of the showing and announce that the feature would be presented at an outdoor location that night. There would be a public invitation for people to accept Christ, and if there was no church in the village, one would be established.

"Hallelujah!" I said. "Let's do it!"

It had been just a few months since I left CBN, and already the pieces to the puzzle were starting to fit. Now if I could only share my enthusiasm with enough people to find the financial support necessary, everything would come together.

One portion of Scripture continually came to me: "For thou shalt go before the face of the Lord to prepare his ways; to give knowledge of salvation unto his people by the remission of their sins, through the tender mercy of our God; whereby the dayspring from on high hath visited us, to give light to them that sit in darkness and in the shadow of death..." (Luke 1:76b-79).

The name given to the project was Dayspring International.

I could see the light dawning on India, China, Africa and the rest of the world. What was that light? Certainly it was the Son of God, the dayspring — the promise of the noonday sun soon to appear. But I could also visualize the powerful light of a projector on a screen shining into the darkened hearts of villagers everywhere.

Over the Edge

Launching a self-sustaining ministry was a new experience for me. In addition to searching God's Word, I turned to see what Christian writers had to say. I read about the death and resurrection of a vision, how to succeed against insurmountable odds, how to activate

God's faith in your life and how to find the power of the Holy Spirit. Would the Lord truly guide my path? If I stepped over the edge into empty space, would God put a foundation under me? Caroline and I were about to find out.

I read several books on entrepreneurship, management and establishing a new enterprise. They all said the same thing, and I was sure it applied to ministry as well as to the world of commerce: You've got to have a good idea, good contacts and capital, and you have to sell and promote. Most important, you have to disregard the critics and *believe* when nobody else does. More than once I called on my personal memories of CBN's miraculous beginnings for strength.

Entering the second year of Dayspring International, the foundation was more like sand than stone. Every day we tottered on the edge. Most operating funds were coming from the small fees I was paid for consulting with other ministries. I borrowed money from close friends and relatives to be paid back later with interest. We were struggling to find the perfect balance between walking by faith and developing a strong organization.

Our modest mailing list contained the names of no more than thirty friends. We rejoiced when a church in Tennessee started sending the ministry $50 each month.

In the fall of 1979 I had written enough letters to fund the purchase of a new Bell & Howell 16mm movie projector. I was absorbed with the idea to return to India to test the concept of outdoor movie showings of *Oceans of Mercy*, followed by an invitation to accept Christ. A small church in Virginia provided $1,800 for the round-trip ticket back to India.

Two major problems faced us. Even though Vijay had approved of the idea of my using the film, the rights had to be negotiated and finalized. Also, I didn't have a copy of the production in a 16mm format. The prints prepared for theaters were in the large 35mm format that required special projectors for viewing.

Vijay told me that only several 16mm copies had been made for a special purpose, and he didn't know how I could possibly get one now. I began an intense search until at last I located one.

I called Komanapalli and said, "I've got the film. Start promoting it; we'll have the first showing tomorrow night."

The Blackest Clouds

The painted sign hanging on the back of a rickshaw told the people about the outdoor movie event. It was in Amalapuram in the state of Andhra Pradesh — a hot, humid area thick with coconut palms, mango trees and lush flowers.

I asked my local hosts to take me to a tailor. They drove to a market where I could find the best in town.

"Sir, I want you to sew me a big movie screen out of bedsheets. I want it twenty feet wide and twenty feet high. And I need it quick."

Within minutes the little man was almost covered with white cloth at his foot-powered sewing machine. He made a beautiful screen.

At the site of the rally we dug holes in the ground, put in two large bamboo poles and strung up the sewn-together sheets. People were already gathering as I tested the new projector, the film and the sound system.

"What are those clouds over there?" I asked. Ernest and I turned to see huge, black swirling clouds coming our way. It looked like a monsoon. Within minutes the palm trees were bending, and I thought the sheets would rip from the bamboo poles. "Lord," I prayed, "I've come all this way, the people are arriving, and now we're going to be washed out. Please, Lord, stop the rain!" But the storm continued to build.

It was just ten minutes until the 8:00 P.M. presentation, and I decided to give the projector one last check to make sure it was lined up perfectly on the screen. When I turned it on, another worker simultaneously plugged in the amplifier, and the projection bulb blew on the Bell & Howell.

"I don't have a spare bulb. It looks as if we're finished before we even begin," I told a helper nearby.

Dejected, I walked down the path where some of my Indian friends were sitting and said, "God's got to do a miracle. He's got to heal a light bulb and shield us with a big umbrella, or we won't be showing this film."

The problem wasn't so monumental after all. I found the projector manual, opened the booklet and read, "If the bulb fails, turn the circuit breaker on after waiting two minutes."

"Lord, let this be it," I said as I finally flipped the switch. I shouted for joy when light flooded the screen. Now we needed a monsoon-sized miracle to divert the storm. The crowd was building fast. First five hundred, then one thousand. The screen itself was a big attraction for the village.

At 8:00 P.M. I turned to Ernest and said, "How many people are here?"

"It looks like about twenty-five hundred," he said, smiling broadly.

Big, hot drops of rain began falling from the dense, blackened sky. I looked up and said, "In the name of Jesus, I command these clouds to leave. I want three hours of clear weather."

The raindrops stopped the moment the projector began.

For the next three hours I did not watch the story on

the makeshift screen. I studied the people. Would their reaction be the same as those in the theater? Would they laugh and cry and be deeply moved by the story? The huge crowd identified with Jesus from beginning to end. I stood in the darkness praising God for what was happening. I was sure this scene would be repeated thousands of times.

At the conclusion of the film, a native minister invited the people of Amalapuram to make a commitment to the Lord Jesus Christ. Hundreds responded — people of every age and occupation; children, mothers, fathers, businessmen, even criminals and prostitutes.

Within five minutes of the service's close, a torrential rain flooded the meeting site.

The next day, at a nearby river, the local pastors held a giant water baptismal service for the new converts. They renounced their many gods and joined the fellowship of Christ.

The Gaddis and Bhojpuris

The concept worked. Ernest Komanapalli and I mapped out a long-range strategy to expand the vision even further. Bible school students would be utilized on our film teams; a multidenominational follow-up and church-planting program would ensure lasting results. Ernest would head Dayspring Enterprises of India, and I would build the resource base and direct the ministry from Virginia Beach.

It was an enormous challenge. Imagine a nation much smaller in size than the United States with five hundred times the number of cities and towns. That's India. Imagine a community with one thousand times the population density of an average U.S. city. That's Bombay, Calcutta or Delhi.

The crowded cities are rife with cholera, malaria, malnutrition and squalor. Any beauty or wealth is dwarfed by the massive poverty. People in rural areas are equally destitute. The typical village home is made of mud and straw — just one or two rooms with a dirt floor. Water comes from the village well. Fewer than 20 percent of the villages have electricity, and most people can't afford fuel. Most try to eke out their daily survival from the land. Some make it. Many do not. Every year there are fourteen million more people competing for the same resources.

We discussed how we could take the film to people who have been called unreachable. The Gaddis, for example, are a nation of eighty thousand people living in the Himalayas. These shepherd people have never heard the gospel story. Or the Bhojpuris, numbering over thirty-five million, considered to be the largest nonevangelized population of India. We could translate the film into their language. An Indian Christ reaching an Indian nation was surely the answer.

Ernest and I determined that the vision must be fulfilled. We vowed that the pace would never slacken. The mission field is too large, the harvest too ripe and the potential too great.

A Look of Disbelief

The immediate difficulty I faced, however, was securing the legal rights to the film. The price we settled on was $103,000. That was a reasonable fee since the project cost about $700,000 to produce. Miraculously, the principal investor, who held the original master print in his vault, agreed to give me power of attorney during a phone call — even though he had never met me. He understood the urgency and sincerity in my voice to bring the gospel to India. Before copies could be made, however, the master would have to be returned to Vijay Chandar.

I told Vijay, "With the stroke of my pen, I can release the film back to you. I'm ready to strike a deal. Please understand that I am not interested in making money. I just want to present the gospel."

He said, "That's no problem. Just give me $15,000 now, and we'll write out a repayment schedule for the remainder."

"I don't think you understand, Vijay," I said, shaking my head. "I don't have any money. But here is what I can do." Vijay looked at me in disbelief while I continued. "I am going to give you a $1,000 check postdated for thirty days. Don't cash it for one month because I don't have it. But I will get it." Then I said, "Here's a second check for $1,000 to be cashed thirty days after that. But remember, I don't have the money yet. Then I'll pay you $5,000 a month until the total amount is paid.

"Vijay," I said, "do you remember how God allowed you to complete the film when it looked impossible?"

"How can I forget?" he replied.

"Well, that's the way the Lord is working again."

Somehow he understood that I meant business.

Is It Going to Work?

The moment we returned to the States, I shared the opportunity with everyone I met — individuals, churches and media ministries. Month after month, miracle after miracle, the funds came in. We met the $1,000 promises then started putting together the $5,000 monthly commitments. However, the pressures were building. Where would I find the funds to pay the rent? How would I provide food for my family?

There was another problem that vexed me greatly. Yes,

there were a few people who caught the vision, but most turned a deaf ear to the need. A friend of my wife's, whose husband was an executive with a large ministry, told her, "I don't really have a burden for all those Indian people. I am just glad my family knows the Lord and are on their way to heaven."

Even more shocking was the statement of another prominent Christian who said, "If people in India want to be saved, they could save themselves."

One day as I sat alone in my little den staring at an empty fireplace, I thought and thought about the project. Is it going to work? Will my sweet Caroline be able to sustain the constant unknown? Is it worth this struggle? Have I made a terrible mistake? My mind was so tormented with doubt that I was almost too paralyzed to pray. At times I felt I was in a trap and God did not want me to go any further. Then I remembered the words of Job, "Though he slay me, yet will I trust in him" (Job 13:15).

I began to claim the words of the old hymn "It Is Well With My Soul" by Horatio G. Spafford:

> When sorrows like sea-billows roll,
>   What ever my lot,
> Thou hast taught me to say,
>   It is well, it is well with my soul.

That night I moved from the sofa and fell prostrate on the tile floor. Pleading my case to God, I said, "Why isn't it any easier? Why have You chosen such a poor vessel to do Your work when there are so many who are truly qualified? Please, Lord, I need Your grace and Your mercy."

The Lord answered, "All I'm asking for is sincerity, faithfulness and a pure heart, and I will bless you." That night I heard again my mother's prayers, saw the pictures on the wall, saw Ernest Komanapalli, Vijay and the hundreds who had come to Christ in Amalapuram.

I stood to my feet, squared my shoulders and said, "Lord, You won't need to find another stone to cry out. I'm called, I'm chosen, and by Your grace I'll be faithful."

FIVE

ONE MORE CRUSADE

Is this John Gilman?" asked the voice on the line.

"Yes, it is," I responded.

"I'm calling from Bill Bright's office in San Bernardino, California. He wants to talk with you about India. He has heard about your film evangelism and wants to meet you. Can we schedule an appointment?"

"You name the time," I said.

It was the winter of 1979, and I had been trying for two months to meet with Bright, head of Campus Crusade for Christ. Every attempt had been fruitless. I was surprised, however, at what he wanted to discuss. My attempts to reach him were on behalf of a completely different project.

I had been appointed national promotions director for Washington for Jesus, a national prayer rally that was to be held in Washington, D.C., in the spring of 1980. Again and again I had suggested that Bright be invited to be the co-chairman for the event. That's why I wanted to see him.

The burden for India was still burning in my heart, but I could see that, unless Christians prayed, repented and interceded for our nation, there might not be an America from which to launch a worldwide evangelism effort.

On the Right Track

A few days later I arrived at the beautiful headquarters of Campus Crusade in the hills near San Bernardino. It was the former Classic Hotel where many famous films had been made. I could hardly go to sleep in that high-ceilinged room, wondering exactly what our discussion would be.

The next morning we met at Bright's home. There were about twelve of his associates in the modest living room. The gracious host opened the conversation by asking, "John, tell me what you're doing in India."

"Dr. Bright, we have the rights to a major motion picture on the life of Jesus that was produced in India and made with all-Indian actors," I said. "It's already been a smash hit in the theaters. But, more than that, thousands are finding Christ."

"What are you going to do with it?" Bright asked.

"We're going to make several hundred prints of the production and mobilize film teams who will go to the villages with generators and big screens. We plan to cover the nation systematically, state by state, district by district, village by village."

His reply was "You're on the right track. That's a good plan."

"I don't have any backing — just a burden to get the job done," I said. "I really don't care who does it or who gets the credit."

Then I made the first of many offers to put the ministry God had given me in the hands of others I thought more capable of carrying it out. "Dr. Bright, I'll be glad to give the film to Campus Crusade and help you evangelize India if that's what God wants me to do."

"John, have you heard about our Genesis Project? We have the life of Christ on film that many call the 'Jesus film.' Currently we are translating it into foreign languages and adding new soundtracks." He told me they had already spent over $5 million on the effort. At that time Bright's organization had not fully developed the program for showing the Jesus movie.

"Yes, I've heard of it," I said. I had met in New York with John Heyman, the producer, and Paul Eshleman, the director of the project, to discuss its use in evangelism.

"Well, what is your opinion?"

I hesitated for a second but told it to him straight. "Dr. Bright, I want to say this very humbly, but I personally don't believe a white Jesus belongs in India."

The film was an excellent one, but I felt it had some real limitations outside a Caucasian or Western culture.

"You've got a strong argument, and we need to talk more about this," he said as he started to close the meeting.

"Dr. Bright, before I go, may I have five minutes to talk with you about the national day of prayer and repentance we're planning for Washington, D.C.?" The burden for Washington for Jesus was swelling in my heart with increasing urgency.

"Yes. Why don't we go to a nearby room?" he suggested.

"Tell Me About It"

Our private meeting was like a "spiritual huddle." He was on the edge of a cot, and I was in a wooden chair. We were both leaning forward with our elbows on our knees as if the next decisions we made would be the difference between winning and losing.

He'd heard about the upcoming event from Pat Robertson but had not yet been asked to be involved.

I searched for the right words to communicate the purpose of the Washington for Jesus concept. "We truly feel that we must call our nation to repentance. Christians from every state should come to the mall and fall to their knees to ask God's mercy on a nation that has so backslidden."

I shared the vision of the committee to see America repent of the anti-God values that were gripping our nation. We prayed for a return to the Judeo-Christian principles that once guided our laws, our government and our culture.

"You know as well as anyone that America is in trouble," I told him. "It's weak, purposeless and has lost its moral fiber. The economy is sinking. We are despised overseas, and our country has turned its back on God." Then I said, "This can be an historic turning point for our nation. We need your help and leadership."

"Who's going to be involved?" he asked.

"Dr. Bright, this is a prayer meeting that should be for *all* of God's people. We're inviting Christians of every persuasion, not just a few charismatics and their friends."

Bright replied, "John, if you can guarantee that those are the goals, I'll join you."

What Does It Mean?

Bright became the co-chairman and played a tremendous part in the success of the event. A short while later I was with him when he called Billy Graham and other key leaders regarding their involvement. I was watching a true missionary statesman at work for his Commander-in-Chief — someone who cared more about the body of Christ than his own ministry.

As the staff of Washington for Jesus and Bright's team began working together, we sensed the awesome responsibility to organize this event around the words found in Scripture: "If My people who are called by My name will humble themselves, and pray and seek My face, and turn from their wicked ways, then I will hear from heaven, and will forgive their sin and heal their land" (2 Chron. 7:14).

Starting at 6:00 A.M. on April 29, 1980, tens of thousands of people poured out of the subways and off buses, planes, trailers, cars and by foot. By early afternoon there were over half a million Christians standing at the great Washington mall. It was the largest Christian gathering in the history of our nation.

Many times during that momentous day the throng knelt and cried out to God to forgive this nation. It was reported in more than three thousand separate newspaper articles and by the media of the world.

"Dr. Bright," I asked as the orderly crowd was leaving, "what do you think this day has meant?"

With the dome of the Capitol sparkling in the golden glow of the evening sun behind him, he said solemnly, "I think this is the most significant day in the history of America since the signing of the Declaration of Independence."

I believe Washington for Jesus was not only a key turning point but a major breakthrough for preparing

America's future role in bringing the gospel to the entire world in this generation.

The encounters with Bill Bright, one of the greatest soul-winners of this century, were a great inspiration to me. I left the event in the nation's capital more determined than ever to reach India and the world with the vision God had given me.

Totally Alone

Yes, we had shown the film in India, and hundreds had come to Christ, but it takes tremendous amounts of money to launch a ministry. By January 1981 we were almost at a standstill.

How could we send out film teams if we couldn't afford the vehicles? How could we show the films when it cost over $1,200 to duplicate just one print? How could I mobilize the Christians in India when I couldn't find the funds to buy a ticket to get there?

As I had done every January since becoming involved in Christian media, I drove to Washington to attend the annual conference of the National Religious Broadcasters. I couldn't afford it, but I went anyway.

Many of my friends were there from across the country and overseas. I wanted to avoid them. I didn't want them to see the discouragement hidden just beneath my veneer of optimism.

"How are you doing, John?" they would ask.

"Just great," I would answer with a smile that didn't quite reach my eyes.

Walking through the corridors of the Washington Sheraton Hotel was an uncomfortable experience. I felt almost in a stupor. There was no real success for Dayspring International to report. I had nothing to "sell" except an enormous vision for the lost. I felt inadequate even to articulate it — embarrassed to share the meager progress I had made.

I could almost hear the people saying under their breath, Why did John ever leave a great ministry like CBN?

Walking through the exhibit hall I felt totally alone despite the thousands of people around me. I questioned God as I moved slowly down a crowded aisle. Why am I here? I wondered. I can't even afford a room in this hotel.

The aisle ended, and I had to decide whether to turn left or right to enter a new area of display booths. In my confusion I just stood there, frozen. If this was a spiritual battle, I was losing.

Finally I walked from the aisle to an escalator. As I did, I heard a voice calling from above. No, it wasn't the Lord, but it might just as well have been. It was Harald Bredesen calling down from the open lobby just above me.

If any person was like Paul the apostle in my life, Bredesen was that man. This Christian visionary and statesman was like a father to me. We had already produced more than one hundred television programs together, including filming an interview in Jerusalem with Prime Minister Menachem Begin. The program later aired on the ABC television network.

A founding board member at CBN, Bredesen had led to Christ hundreds of personalities in entertainment, business and government. Since 1966 he had taken me on as one of those many young people he would love and encourage to be all they could be for the Lord.

"I Want You to Have It"

As the escalator came to the top, Bredesen walked briskly over to me and yelled loud enough for everyone within a hundred feet to hear, "Praise God! It's so good to see you, Tim!" (He knew my name but always liked to refer to our relationship as "Paul and Timothy.")

The short, stocky, steel-jawed man was, as usual, brimming with excitement. With his arm tightly around my waist and his head bent forward, he pulled me along quickly as we walked. He once told me this was how he got his exercise.

"Why don't you come with me to the hotel room? There are a few of us gathering there just to have fellowship."

I was overjoyed to be with Harald. It was comforting to realize I was being encouraged by one of the great Christians of our time.

Several people were already there when we arrived. Harald pulled off his shoes and sprawled on the bed — hands behind his head — praising God out loud. All the chairs were taken, so I sat down on the floor, my back against the dresser.

Harald, as he always does, began probing me for the truth about how I was really getting along. I shared a little of my frustration over having this enormous vision for reaching the villagers in India with the powerful tool of film, but not knowing how to make it a reality.

After a few minutes of conversation, Harald rolled over on his side and fumbled for his wallet. He pulled it out of his back pocket and threw it across the room — right at me!

"What are you doing that for?" I said as I caught it.

"Look inside," he said. "Tell me what's in there."

When I looked, there was a hundred dollar bill and two one dollar bills.

"Go ahead and take it out," said Harald. "I want you to have it. All of it."

"Harald, I can't take your money."

Although I knew how often Bredesen gave away anything he had for the gospel's sake, I wasn't about to take advantage of his generosity. Plus, my pride didn't want me to accept anything in front of the others who were still in the room.

Harald insisted, "You must take that money. God wants you to have it, brother." I was deeply moved — not by the fact that the Lord had just performed a financial miracle for me, but because a man of God would so instantly give everything he had for the gospel.

How could I do less?

A Tidal Wave

I returned from Washington as if my battery had just been jump-started on a cold winter morning. When I opened the mail, I could hardly believe the reports from India. Even without finances, native pastors were finding ways to take a scratchy print of the film and show it in the villages. Week after week the letters kept coming. Salvation reports were soon totaling into the thousands, then over ten thousand.

When I called Ernest Komanapalli, he said, "You need to come over here quickly. Something is happening! I believe God is about to bring millions of people to the Lord through this film."

Oceans of Mercy was becoming a tidal wave.

I returned to India to find people everywhere ready to join the team. The first showing we had in the slums of Bombay attracted some three thousand people — plus plenty of pigs and chickens. Our screen was a bedsheet stretched between the second floors of two shacks near a little square. An open sewer ran through the area, and the ground was wet and spongy. In the midst of that filth, hundreds came forward for salvation.

My enthusiasm for the vision became contagious. God

sent funds from unexpected sources. The ministry friends grew from thirty to three hundred and then to three thousand! Pat Robertson shared with his television audience what was happening, and people across America began to undergird the project. He said, "John, if you continue on this course, all of that great nation will be evangelized indeed!"

I was able to tell people that Dayspring's strategy is not a solution looking for a problem. Film is the most persuasive and pervasive tool of communication on earth. And in India people are crazy about films. Other methods of evangelism have their place, but none is more effective in such a short period of time.

It became clear that in less than three hours we could impart both an awareness of Christianity and an understanding of the fundamentals of the gospel. When I saw how unreached people could grasp the personal implication of God's mercy, I wanted to duplicate a thousand films and buy a thousand vans.

Like Paul, our team leaders experienced new converts at the first presentation of the gospel.

We were seeing more than converts, however. The follow-up program we established was resulting in new churches springing up week after week. Before long many of the new Christians became propagators of the gospel themselves. One man, O.C.K. Balai, a businessman from Madra Pradesh, is now part of the same film team that won him to Christ.

The greater the victories were, however, the greater the needs seemed to be. The film had been translated into the Hindi language, and Dayspring needed $85,000 to obtain the rights so that we could establish mobile film teams to reach millions more with the gospel. We also needed dozens of film prints, transportation and so much more. If we had $85,000, it could be launched immediately. But that was an enormous mountain for Dayspring to climb.

Stephen's Prayer

"Boys, Daddy is going out on the road, and I've got to have $85,000 in thirty days or we will lose the opportunity to get these rights. I'm going to be visiting people to ask for their help, and I'm not coming back until I get it."

It was the fall of 1982, and we became convinced that launching a film ministry in India's most widely spoken language, Hindi, was our number-one priority. I gathered the family around me at our home in Virginia Beach and asked them to pray. We stood in a circle in the hallway between two bedrooms — my wife and our two sons, John and Stephen.

I said, "Stephen, would you ask God to give Daddy $85,000 so we can get the film into Hindi?"

"No, Daddy," he said. "What if you don't get it? I don't want to be responsible."

"Well, would you pray for the Lord to give me a safe trip and for God's favor to be on me?"

When he finished praying, I asked God for the $85,000.

On that journey I went to the first person, the second and then the third. None of them was able to help. It was the same answer from the next, and the next. The eleventh person to whom I presented the need said, "I can't help you, but the fellow in the next room might be able to."

I went and presented my story. He said, "I can't do anything personally, but I'm on the board of Mark Buntain's ministry. I believe he can do something for you."

To anyone involved in missions in India, the name Mark Buntain is a household word. His Mission of Mercy to Calcutta built scores of churches, fed hundreds of thousands of starving children and built hospitals and orphanages. He was often affectionately referred to as "St. Mark."

"Right now he's in Missouri, where he's been very ill. I'll call him and tell him about you," said the trustee.

"You can also tell him I'm on my way to see him," I added.

I got a plane ticket to St. Louis and rented a car. He was in Columbia, Missouri, about two hours west of the city. On the way I stopped at a phone booth to get the exact directions.

"Dr. Buntain," I said with considerable awe, "this is John Gilman. Did you get a call from one of your board members about me? He said he was going to call and tell you what I'm doing in India."

"No," he said. "No one has called about you. But I want you to come on down. Please come. I want to hear about India."

He was alone in his apartment. His fingers were curled and twitching with pain from a spinal operation. I could tell he was enduring immense suffering.

As I told him about our film, he stood to his feet and paced the small room. Back and forth. Back and forth. He started weeping and praising God. Then he said, "John, if I had $85,000, I'd give it to you right now."

But at that moment I didn't care if he didn't have a dime: The Lord had put me at the feet of this incredible missionary for a divine purpose.

"But I do have $35,000 that the board of my ministry wants me to use for crusades in India," he said. "Oh, if I could have just one more crusade! But I'm just too ill to go. Can you come out to Tacoma, Washington, to the next meeting of our board? I'm going to ask them to give you the $35,000 for the Hindi film."

"I'll be there, Dr. Buntain."

At that important meeting, his board asked dozens of

questions about our vision to reach India with the gospel. Then they said, "Let us pray about this tonight. We'll let you know our decision tomorrow."

The next day one of the board members said, "We want to help. We are going to give you $35,000 now and loan you $50,000 so you can start the work immediately."

When I came bouncing through the door after being gone only fifteen days, little Stephen said, "We prayed pretty good, didn't we, Daddy?"

"You Must Be Kidding!"

My conversations with Mark Buntain and other great men of God have been eye-opening. Missionaries have been frustrated by their inability to communicate the gospel they love to tell. In almost every case the great barriers are cultural.

That's why it is important to have the gospel presented by the people of the nation to be reached. Having an all-Indian cast on film is vital, and so is the fact that it was shot on location in that country. When the audience looks up at the screen and sees Jesus heal the leper, they say, "This must be true. These are our people telling the story." Many times, after a film showing, they ask, "What village does Jesus come from?"

They are ready to be taught.

We also insist that every member of our film team be a native pastor, evangelist or lay person. Someone asked me, "John, it must be exciting to stand up after the film and give an invitation or greet the people."

"You must be kidding," I said.

When I go to the location of an *Oceans of Mercy* showing, I stay in the van — sometimes slumped down in the front seat — until it is completely dark so the people won't see me. Only then do I get out, standing in the shadows to see the people respond to the film. When it is almost over, I get back in the vehicle until the crowd has departed. Why should a foreigner become a barrier to people about to accept Christ?

"What's he saying? What's he saying?" I often ask a native missionary with me in the van as the invitation is being given. There's no comparison to the invitations given in American evangelical churches.

Here's what one of our team members said to the vast film audience: "Friends, our holy books tell us that without the shedding of blood there is no forgiveness of sins. But it is not the shedding of the blood of pigs, chickens and goats which can save us, but the blood of Someone very special. And that Someone you have seen tonight. He is God's Son, who shed His own blood for your sin. Will you receive God's sacrifice for you and not shed the blood of animals again?"

The audience understands. They respond.

In the early days of missions there was no other way but to export the gospel to the world. Missionaries had to live among the natives — winning their confidence by learning their language and customs. Often, years passed without a single convert. Considering the odds, they did a remarkable job, leaving behind an army of committed native Christians. Perhaps that is why we are now seeing converts in foreign nations at an unprecedented rate.

Mark Buntain is in heaven. He will soon be surrounded by millions of Hindi-speaking souls because of his investment. Yes, there was "one more crusade" — and it still continues.

"I WANT TO BE LIKE HIM"

Worship, O Cow,
   To thy tail-hair, and to thy hooves,
Both gods and mortal men,
   Depend for life and being upon the Cow.

How do you reach a people who believe in such Hindu doctrine? Where do you build a bridge to those who revere sacred cows and animals that supposedly possess great powers?

The religion called Hinduism, to which about 85 percent of India subscribes, holds a set of beliefs that is as far from Christianity as any you will ever find. It tells the people they must be reincarnated back to this earth innumerable times until they reach a state of perfection. The ladder, however, does not only go up. If they fail in any way, the gods may punish them by having them return as a member of a lower caste, or even as an animal or insect. Hindus believe that every person deserves their present plight because of the *karma*, or law of moral consequence.

The caste system is a fiercely guarded tenet of the Hindu religion. It is made up of five major castes, including the untouchables (or "outcasts"), into which one is born based on his behavior in a previous life. The gods have no control over this. It is a consequence of one's own actions.

Hinduism is one of the world's oldest religions. It has no founder and was begun sometime around 1500 B.C. by Aryan invaders who mixed their Vedic religion with the existing practices and beliefs of the natives. Some say that Hinduism is not a religion at all, and that it is impossible to define. There is no central authority, no hierarchy, no claim of divine revelation, and it has no strict moral code. It is a tolerant belief and easily accommodates other religions. It has been criticized as "standing for everything, and thus, for nothing."

This fascinating belief is both simple and complex. Across India you will find gurus sitting for hours trying to explain its subtleties to disciples.

Bloodthirsty Kali

What about a supreme being? There is none. There are 330 million gods, with the chief one, Brahman, not really a god at all but an "it" — an ultimate reality, impersonal and indefinable.

What does a poor, starving, wretched Hindu Indian have to look forward to? The highest objective in existence is an eventual and final union with Brahman through karma after perhaps eons of reincarnations.

One of the goddesses, Kali, is the Hindu personification of evil and destruction, the bloodthirsty deity of the cult of Shakti, and considered to be the "divine mother." She is considered the goddess of epidemics and earthquakes, of floods and storms. In many temples you can find images of her with blood dripping from her mouth.

Kali demands blood sacrifices from her believers. She demands the offering but gives absolutely nothing in return. In former times human sacrifices were made to her, but now goats are used. It is a rather common sight to watch a goat being decapitated publicly at a temple. The little animal's neck is placed in a three-inch-high wooden post built for the purpose. Then, as someone holds the goat's hind legs, the curved sword of the executioner quickly falls, severing the neck in one stroke. As the blood spews, the priests beat their drums wildly and shout, "Jai ma Kali, Jai ma Kali" — "Glory to Mother Kali, glory to Mother Kali."

Hinduism is given the credit for giving birth to three other religious factions: Jainism, Buddhism and Sikhism. Also in India, Islam accounts for about 10 percent of the population. Hindus and Moslems regularly clash over territorial issues.

What has Hinduism produced for its followers? Fear, despair, conflict, emptiness — the product of silent gods, stone images in temples who demand favor but who return nothing. It's a theology devoid of love.

If there ever was a place of hopelessness, it is India. Whatever Hinduism is, the entire nation, economy and culture are within its grip. So are the souls of its people.

Jesus surely must have considered it when He spoke

of "a field ripe unto harvest." Yet to the Lord be glory! No circumstances — no deception, no religion — is too difficult for Him to penetrate. The stories of transformed lives because of *Oceans of Mercy* would fill the pages of countless volumes. By the grace of God we have presented the film to more than thirty million people in India. By the power of God more than three million have come to Christ. The Dayspring International offices have received thousands of letters from these new Christians. Every individual tells a marvelous story of the transforming mercy of God.

Veda, the Hindu Priest

As a youngster, Veda wanted to be a Hindu priest. He worked hard as a teenager to prove worthy of the priesthood and to obtain the favor of the gods. He eventually became the holy man of the temple in his village that worshipped the Hindu god of fertility.

A large number of people would visit Veda's shrine, more than would come to any other in the area. They would bring offerings of grain or flower petals and pray for rain, good soil or good crops. Every morning Veda would open the temple with the loud clanging of bells and the burning of incense.

For twenty-eight years he went through this same ritual, praying to statues and paintings that never offered him anything in return. For nearly three decades Veda made empty chants to them — chants to inanimate objects. Then something happened to him. Here are Veda's own words:

> Being a Hindu priest was something that gave me power and satisfaction. People depended on me to gain for them the good will of the

gods. But somewhere along the way I realized that people were looking to me for something I could not give. However, I continued to go through the motions in order to keep the gods from striking me dead.

One day a van pulled into the field next to my temple. The man asked if he could plug his electrical cord into my outlet. It seemed harmless enough, so I let him. The film they showed in the street that night was about Jesus Christ and how He provided the supreme sacrifice — that no other sacrifice would be needed to make me clean. During the scenes of the crucifixion, I began to cry and couldn't stop.

Veda's life was changed forever. But he is not the only Hindu priest this has happened to. There are many others — all over India — who have seen the film and now understand about the one great sacrifice that was made for everyone, everywhere. No sacrifice would ever need to be made again. They learned that God *gives* life instead of taking it.

It Happened to Shamar

In another village a farmer named Shamar told his story.

Life for me and my family has been hard. We had a small farm until last spring when a flood came and destroyed everything. Our farm was totally lost, and we had nothing left. My wife was expecting our third child, but we couldn't feed the two we had.

One morning the children were arguing,

and the heat was unbearable for my wife. With my head aching and spinning, I walked out of our house that didn't have any doors. I walked toward the river. By the time I reached the water, I had made up my mind to kill myself by jumping into the river and drowning. At least my wife could then take the children and go to live with her father.

Somehow it didn't matter to me that by Hindu custom I would be doomed to return to earth as an insect or some despised animal. I didn't want to leave my wife and children, but I saw no other way out. Something kept me from ending my life, and I walked back to our little house. I thought, I'll do it tonight.

That evening the village was unusually busy. Everyone seemed to be heading toward a flat, grassy area on the other side of the river, so I followed to see what was happening. It was a film being shown, and I said to myself, The river can wait. I had never heard about Jesus before this film. I could hardly believe my eyes. He performed miracles and even raised the dead. This Jesus was not put off by the darkest problem or the worst situation. Instead He turned the darkness into light. That's what He did for me that night, and since then, for my wife too. A new church has started in my village, and we all encourage each other. Thank God for that film and for giving my family a new life.

"I Was a Terror"

Shri Lawrence was an alcoholic on Pizhala Island near

Cochin, on the southwest coast of India. "In my profession of selling shrimp, I earned enough money to support my wife and two children, but I spent everything on liquor. My life was miserable, and I was a terror to those around me."

Then something happened. "A man by the name of N.T. Thomas came to our island with his film team to show the film about Jesus. It was through this picture that I came to know the innocent Lamb of God who was slain for my sins. That night I accepted Christ as my personal Savior."

Shri gave up his habit of drinking, was baptized and joined a Christian church. "I am indebted to the film team who showed me the way to salvation."

Hell's Garbage Cans

Shandar and George had families, but finding food became almost impossible for them. They made the decision, as many do, to become thieves. Thievery is a widespread occupation in India. Crime is so rampant that the police overlook much of it. However, Shandar and George were arrested because someone was killed during one of their robberies.

The men soon discovered why India's prisons are called "hell's garbage cans." Many do not get out alive. Conditions are horrible, because the prisons are designed to be a deterrent to crime. After being released from prison, their wives rejected them because of the disgrace the men had brought to the family. They slept on the streets with no place else to go. But after all of that, they still had not been cured of their thievery.

One night they saw a crowd of people gathering, and they decided this would be a good opportunity for them. The crowd had gathered after a van passed by inviting people to come to a free film. Here is how George described it:

> It was something we could not pass up. We were sure most of the village people would be there, and we decided that most of their homes would be empty, and we could go and rob them. We stood in the back.
>
> As soon as the film started, we saw that this was no ordinary film. It was about a man named Jesus. He was able to change people. He could change anyone who asked Him. I had the strangest feeling. Both George and I stayed after the film and asked Jesus to change us. We wanted to be like Him.

Shandar and George started looking for work the next day. They are back with their families and are involved with the newly established church in their village. It is evident to others that if Jesus Christ can change a hardened Indian criminal, He can change anyone.

Women of the Street

Roga and Anna lived as prostitutes on the squalid streets of Calcutta. It's a way of life — a means of survival for many. For the two women, it was the only life they knew. Their minds and feelings were numb from their daily routine. It was how their mothers had lived, and their mothers' mothers. No one had ever told them there was a purpose to life or that anyone cared. Roga and Anna came to the showing of *Daya Sagar* one night. They knew the title meant "oceans of mercy," but they did not know why.

The two prostitutes soon discovered the meaning of the

title. They were wide-eyed with amazement when Jesus showed mercy to the woman caught in adultery and when He had compassion for the poor and the sick. Their questions about purpose in life were answered when they heard Jesus say, "When you drink the water that I give, you'll never thirst again."

Roga and Anna joined about five hundred others that night who committed their lives to Christ.

A Family of Thieves

For generations the family of K. Ramaiah was involved in thievery and crime. He said, "We were idol-worshippers and sacrificed animals to our gods." His brothers were in and out of prison, and one "committed suicide by putting his head under a train." Says Ramaiah, "Though we worshipped many gods, we had no peace. And due to my friendship with thieves, I was always in great trouble."

While Ramaiah was suffering from a severe illness, a Dayspring film team came to his village. "It was near my residence, and I sat very close to the screen — observing the film with a heavy heart." When he saw Christ dying on the cross, he was greatly moved and gave his heart to Jesus. "I accepted Him as my personal Savior. That night the Lord gave me peace of mind."

"I Wept"

In the East Godavari district lives G. Parkasham and his wife, Suseela. "My wife used to attend church, but I didn't like it. Instead I would stay home and drink. Then I would beat her when she returned from the house of worship. Many times she tried to tell me about Jesus, but I would reject her and tell her to stop talking about

Christ."

One day the local pastor brought a Dayspring film team to the village. "Suseela forced me to see that picture. Before long, tears were coming out of my eyes. The scene of the Lord on the cross moved my heart greatly. I wept and confessed my sins before the Lord. Now my wife and I are preaching the gospel in our surrounding area."

Manta's New Covenant

Daily you could find her at the Hindu temple. Manta would walk to the temple to make a blood sacrifice to the goddess Kali to try to appease her. A little animal would be beheaded, and the blood would be offered to this goddess of evil and destruction.

It was not unusual. There seems to be something instinctive in pagan cultures that blood is associated with sacrifice for sin. It has been a widespread practice since the beginning of time. Manta did not know it, but she was a victim of Satan, who takes a spiritual truth and perverts it for his purposes. She had no way of knowing that the Son of God had shed His blood and provided that sacrifice one time for all.

Manta discovered this great truth when she went to a film showing in her village. That night she claimed Jesus' own blood as her atonement. At that instant she was set free from the superstition and fear of Kali. By believing in Jesus and accepting what He did for her, she entered into the new covenant, a blood covenant with God Himself.

> In Him we have redemption through His blood, the forgiveness of sins, according to the riches of His grace (Eph. 1:7).

He has delivered us from the power of darkness and translated us into the kingdom of the Son of His love, in whom we have redemption through His blood, the forgiveness of sins (Col. 1:13-14).

A New Source of Light

Andrus is an elderly man who all his life had lived in dread and superstition. One evening while walking on a dirt road near his village, he saw a strange glow of light over the hill ahead of him.

The man approached the top of the hill with a mixture of caution and anxiety. He then saw the source of the light. It was from a large square of white cloth in a crowd of people. As he got closer he could tell they were all watching a film on this piece of cloth. Andrus joined the crowd and "found the Messiah." His life now has the true light that brightens men's hearts.

Every day the stories keep coming.

• Mrs. Kunji said, "I am a Hindu lady. During the crucifixion scene I began to weep as never before. I went forward and accepted Jesus as my personal Savior."

• A young woman wrote, "I raised my hand when the invitation was given. What else could I do when He died in my place?"

• A man named Mahalaxmi said, "Along with hundreds of people I saw the story of Jesus with my own eyes and heard it with my own ears. I accepted Jesus. To me it is better to see this film once instead of hearing ten messages."

• A girl in Bombay said, "I came to the film, but I never would have gone to a church."

• John, an Indian pastor in the village of Amalapuram said, "Sometimes I had to travel two or three days just to

minister to two or three people at the most. We just had
to do what we could. Then one day this film came. It was
unbelievable — two thousand, three thousand, five thousand came out to see a presentation on the life of Jesus.
The response was overwhelming."

A New Temple

This letter recently crossed my desk.

> My name is Hanuman. My God is 'Genesn.'
> My house is a temple for our idol. Outside my
> house I engraved our beliefs on a stone and
> fixed it on the wall. I perform Puja (worship),
> Manthra (witchcraft) and all other customs of
> our tradition every day to attract people to our
> idol. One day nobody came to my house. I
> went out to know the whereabouts of the peo-
> ple.
>   In the outskirts of our village I found a huge
> gathering of people viewing a film. I ap-
> proached the crowd. It was the film *Daya
> Sagar*. I keenly observed the film. It was won-
> derful. My heart was shocked when I saw the
> crucifixion of Jesus. I came to know that Jesus
> is the only way for the salvation of my sins. I
> gave my heart to Him. I invited the film unit
> workers to my house. They stayed in my house
> and prayed for me. Now my house is a temple
> for Jesus.

A Transformed Family

Another letter came from a man in the village of
Amdinagar.

The great film *Daya Sagar* did a miracle in our family. My neighbor, Mr. Gangaram, asked me to see the film in our town. It was 8:00 P.M. My son is bedridden with a chronic disease. One of my daughters is dumb. Our family is very large, with much suffering due to several struggles.

We entirely lost our hope in life and decided to die by suicide. But after seeing the film a new hope came to my life. The sweet loving words of Jesus started ringing in my heart. I asked Jesus to heal my bedridden son and also give peace in my family. That very moment my son raised up from the bed and has taken food after ten days. Our whole family believed in Jesus. Please pray for us.

Is it worth the effort to bring the story of the cross to the villages of the world? New names are being written in the book of life: Veda, Shamar, Shri, Shandar, Roga, Ramaiah, Manta, Hanuman and countless more.

The light has only begun to shine as we present Christ to the world. Under starlit skies I can see people everywhere looking up to say, "I want to be like Him. I want to follow the innocent Man."

A typical billboard in India advertises a showing of *Daya Sagar* (Oceans of Mercy). The film was produced with all native Indian actors.

This vivid portrayal on film of the life, death and resurrection of Christ has helped win millions of Indians to Christ during the past ten years.

John Gilman (center) stands with a group of Indian film team leaders.

A Dayspring International van arrives at a village for a showing of *Daya Sagar*.

Pastor Samuel, a well-known Christian minister in India, receives his copy of *Daya Sagar* from John Gilman (see Pastor Samuel's story in chapter 10).

Village children gather in curiosity as a movie screen is suspended between two rough wooden poles.

Crowds in India react with sorrow and dismay when they see
Jesus crucified on film. At one showing people throughout the
audience shouted, "They're killing an innocent man!"

Audience members raise their hands and pray to accept Christ after a showing of *Daya Sagar*.

Native Christian leaders baptize new converts in an Indian river.

A local group of Christians dedicate a new church building which was sponsored and built by Dayspring International.

The John Gilman family: John Jr., Caroline, John and Stephen.

SEVEN

ON THE
SILVER SCREEN

The men and women who take the film into the villages often do so at the risk of their lives. If the book of Acts were being written today, it would be filled with their courageous stories.

"Let's kill this man!" shouted a band of Hindu fundamentalists as they disrupted the showing of *Oceans of Mercy* to an audience of three thousand.

Ernest Komanapalli tells the story of the six men who suddenly burst on the scene. "They battered the projector, destroyed the film and began to physically beat four other film unit members.

"They grabbed Pastor Shadrack and took him from the open field, saying, 'At least we should kill one man.' He was bleeding on the roadside as they attempted to kill him."

Ernest recounted, "The angry Hindus saw a light coming down the road and took off. But it was just a noisy motorized rickshaw. The driver heard the groanings of Pastor Shadrack and took him to a hospital, where he was confined for a month."

Within a few weeks of his release, Shadrack was taking the film back to the villages. "I am ready to die for the Lord," he said. "I must show them and tell them about Jesus."

They've Never Heard

As you are reading these pages there are men walking with projectors strapped to their backs to take the gospel to the people. One of our teams has only one bicycle, but somehow they manage to tie on a projector, portable generator and three people to reach the villages. Half of their time is spent pushing the bike and the equipment up the hills.

The village of Ragupalli can only be reached by foot. It is located miles up in the hills where no roads have been built. Yet a Dayspring film unit was determined to reach the people. As they hiked through the mountains with the equipment, the word spread that something very important was about to happen.

That evening nearly twenty-five hundred people gathered. They came from small villages throughout the area. Most of them had never seen a movie projector — or heard the name of Jesus.

Our files are filled with reports of teams that travel five or six hours to reach one village to present *Oceans of*

Mercy. They don't get home until dawn. One film evangelist takes his equipment by horseback to share the good news.

No barrier seems too great to stop those with a passion to present the visual message of Christ. A native film team leader wrote, "Gaddabavalasa is a tribal village situated on the top of mighty hills. A thick forest separates the groups of huts that line the hilltops. The people who inhabit these small dwellings are spirit worshippers with no knowledge of Jesus.

"To reach the village," the letter continued, "we had to cross a lake on a small boat with all of our equipment. The people ran to welcome us and carried our projector and generator for twenty miles to the village. It was a tiring experience, but the effort was worth it.

"The tribal people enthusiastically asked about Jesus and His wonderful miracles. They watched the film — their eyes filled with excitement and awe. And the message reached their hearts. Many of them now hike miles every Sunday to nearby villages where churches have been established. We're thankful we managed to reach them."

Another team leader wrote, "We're now showing our film in the Manipur State — along the border of Burma. We are spreading the good news of Jesus throughout this rugged terrain, without getting a complete night's rest. Since there are no proper roads in this state, we are often forced to put the equipment on a raft or tie it on bicycles as we journey through rough areas. Yet we are reaching a variety of different tribal people, and God is allowing us to make a difference in their lives."

Inciting the Villagers

Since the beginning of the film ministry in India our

goal has been to supply mini-vans and Jeeps to our teams. Our fleet of vehicles is increasing, but the demand greatly outnumbers the supply.

Often transportation is vital in more ways than one.

One of the film unit leaders wrote, "Zingerbail was a totally unreached area where the name of Christ had never been heard. The entire village came to the film showing, but the local military was actively trying to turn the population against us. They incited some of the villagers to leave before the film was over.

"At one point we thought we would be stoned," he recounted. "We had the Jeep in reverse and ready to go. However, the Lord gave us a great victory. Almost all the remaining villagers responded by raising their hands when the invitation was given. They came forward to accept Christ. We prayed for each of them and exhorted them to continue in the Lord."

In spite of the persecution, he wrote, "The beginning of a strong church was planted in the village that night."

Every Dayspring film team member has experienced harassment and abuse for proclaiming Christ. One wrote, "We are working in an area dominated by Hindus. To these people anyone claiming to be a Christian is an outcast and looked down upon — only allowed to do menial labor.

"In one village they warned us not to show anything about Christianity, but we went about our work. Then, before we could project the film on the screen, someone cut our power cord, and they ran off with our public address system. When we asked for it back, the men manhandled the film operator and tore off his shirt. All we could do was collect the rest of our belongings and walk to the edge of the village to pray."

Prayer worked. "After about fifteen minutes," he said, "a man named Surayya came to us with the stolen sound system and apologized. The man told me, 'The young people of the village were excited about the announcement of the film and want to see it, so we will let them.' "

Immediately the young people came to help set up the screen — right in front of the local Hindu temple. They had convinced the village elders to allow the film to be shown.

"After the showing," said the film team leader, "some of the young men and women came forward to say that they understood the love of Jesus and the sacrifice He had made. They believed that He is the Savior of sinners and asked us to pray with them."

Plotting to Kill

Often the people who are violently opposed to the gospel are touched by something they never expected.

Recently we received a letter from a man in India's state of Madhya Pradesh. "I was brought up in a staunch Hindu family. We worshipped the gods of nature — wind, fire, water and earth. Often we walked on fire to prove our faith. When the film was brought to our town, the Mana Village, I was so opposed to it that I plotted to kill the operator.

"I went to the showing determined to make havoc, but fell asleep due to heavy drinking of liquor made of ganja leaf. I woke up when the film showed Jesus dying on the cross. I gave my heart to Him. My entire family has now been changed."

Persecution comes not only from Hindus. Political factions, especially the communists, often become furious when they hear that the message of Christ is coming to a village.

According to a mobile film team leader from the state

of Kerala, in the village of Ponnuruthy "we obtained permission for showing the movie on a barren piece of ground. The owner of the land was a communist, and we did not go into detail regarding the contents of the film to be presented."

That omission proved to be a mistake. "In the middle of the film," wrote the native evangelist, "the man who owned the property caused a big disturbance and ordered that the film be stopped — and that we get off his property immediately."

Fortunately, his word was not the last. "The public was incensed by his outrage and settled the matter with him, right on the spot."

A similar event happened in the village of Sanjeevardy. The film unit manager said, "Some angry communists were troubled from the moment we entered the village. They would not allow us to show the film. After trying for a long period of time to cooperate with them, we went to get a meal at the local hotel — only to be kicked out. We were not even able to find a place to sleep. No one allowed us to come in off the dirty streets."

When a group of the villagers learned what was happening, they put such pressure on the communists that the situation was turned completely around. "The people so desired to see the film that those who had been protesting suddenly began to treat us with genuine hospitality. It was miraculous. At the showing that night, many accepted Christ."

Time after time the villagers have come to the rescue of our film teams. In southwest India, a native evangelist told us, "We were showing the production in a place called Kakanad. Right in the middle of the movie a man who claimed to be the secretary of the local administration came to me and demanded that the projector be stopped. The moment the light went out, the people knew what had happened. They intervened on our behalf, and the administrator was forced to leave." Again, that night people found the Lord.

The Wobbly Picture

"What am I to do?" Subier asked.

His dark brown eyes seemed to be pleading with mine as we looked at each other over the projector.

I had traveled with him and the Dayspring mobile film team several hundred miles in two Jeeps and an old rented car. We arrived at the top of a mountain near a rain forest in the state of Orissa. Now the film wouldn't work properly.

The day had been rough enough, and now this. Actually we were fortunate to have made the trip in one piece. The car constantly overheated — we stopped twelve times to get water from streams that flowed alongside the road. As the sun was going down, one of the Jeeps had a problem with the gas line. We got out and tried to fix it with a tiny flashlight.

Those who knew something about motor repair continued to work on it while I sat down to rest on a stone wall at the edge of the road. With the Jeep fixed, we made it as far as the road would take us, then hiked back into the woods to set up the projector and screen in the darkness.

The journey for the audience was just as difficult. Many had walked up to 120 kilometers to watch *Oceans of Mercy*. Some came so far that they had to spend the previous night sleeping outside under the stars.

We put the film into the projector, and it would not work properly. The picture was wobbly, and the sound was garbled. The longer the film continued, the worse the problem became.

I looked over at Subier; he was trying to hold the "gate" down on the projector so the film would feed properly — another man spun the reel around with his finger so he could wind up the film as it came out of the machine.

When I looked at the movie, I couldn't believe what I saw. Six or seven of every ten sprocket holes were torn. Subier had shown his print of the film over eight hundred times. The *maximum* is usually five hundred showings. Yet, even on this night, with the film in such a broken-down condition, many people gave their lives to Jesus.

When Subier said, "What am I going to do?" I determined that I would take whatever steps were necessary to see that his team had a fresh print of the film.

"Please Don't Stop!"

Showing *Oceans of Mercy* outdoors has presented many challenges. One film team went to an area in a mountain region. The wind was so fierce it caused the film to twist and break as it entered the projector.

Many of our mobile film team leaders have had experiences similar to the one we had at our first film showing in Amalapuram. That's the night I had to pray that God would hold back a giant thunderstorm — and He did.

One evangelist wrote, "We were presenting the film in the village of Amabedkar Nagar when all of a sudden the skies opened up, and it began to rain. It was a very large gathering, with nearly seven thousand people present. When the crowd felt the wind and the rain, they knew it was probably the end of the showing. But they begged us, 'Please don't stop the story of Jesus. God will take care of the situation.' And they gathered to put their umbrellas over the projector.

"No one moved away from the meeting place," he related, "although the rain turned into a downpour. Everyone was drenched, but they continued to watch. Then, at the point in the film where the wind and rain are calmed by Jesus, the rain around us also stopped! The faith of the people was inspired. Even the Muslims and the Hindus praised God for this miracle."

Beyond the Blitz

Tonight, thousands of Indians will gather to see *Oceans of Mercy* — from Tamil Nadu in the south to Uttar Pradesh in the north. There will be showings in Himachal Pradesh State, in Orissa, in Bihar and many other areas. The film has already been translated into the major languages of India: Hindi, Bengali, Kannada, Oriya, Telugu, Tamil, Marathi, Malayalam.

In a country where 70 percent of the people are illiterate, a motion picture is the most effective means of presenting the gospel. Reaching large masses of people is critical — there is only one Christian worker for every 472,000 people in India. There are simply not enough people for one-on-one evangelism.

From the beginning of the ministry, I realized God's perfect plan was not a blitz but the establishment of the body of Christ in every nation or people group. As we moved closer to the heart of God regarding world missions, we made a commitment to much more than film evangelism. We are working tirelessly with the leadership of many church groups to build Christian fellowships and even physical buildings among the nearly three thousand nations of people in India who do not have a body of believers among them.

The letters we receive from mobile film team leaders tell the story.

From the coastal village of Ganipeswaram: "We are able to reach many interior villages for the first time with

115

the gospel. We have started a worship center here and appointed a permanent pastor, David Raju."

From East India: "On the outskirts of Vijayawada is a slum called Payakapurnam. People who went to the film for the first time wanted to see it again and again to build up their faith in Jesus. Now a new church has been established, and John Babu is the pastor."

In a communist-controlled village the village chief allowed the film to be shown to almost thirty-five hundred people. Nearly four hundred gave their hearts to Christ, and a church was built.

They Came by Ox Cart

Recently I read a detailed report of what is taking place in an area just south of Madras. I glanced through the pages and saw the numbers of people being saved — 50, 70, 120, 180, 200, 300, 350. One village after another is being changed by the message of the gospel. In the small community of Vriddachalam only three hundred people came to see the film, but more than half of them — 180 to be exact — indicated a firm decision to accept Christ.

Churches are being established in these villages. In a place called Cheran Colony in Tiruppur, one of the new converts opened her home to hold church meetings every week. A pastor from a nearby town conducts the services.

In Ulunderpet the film was so requested that it was shown seven times. It was followed by a short crusade, and a church was born with seventy-five people attending on the very first day. Without the film it would normally have taken a missionary two or three years to establish a church of this size in the area.

Even the new congregations write to express their thanks.

The leader of one church said, "Our village of Middenagaram is in a remote forest area where no bus or van could reach. But these children of God loved us and came by ox cart to bring us the movie on the life of Jesus. We heard the message of the gospel through them. After seeing the movie, nearly thirty of us believed in the Lord Jesus Christ as our Savior."

Another wrote, "We thank you for sending us the film and for showing us the true and only God. We began to attend a church that was over fifteen miles from our village. We were baptized in water at this church and attended there for several weeks, even though it was far away and we did not have any way to get there, except to walk. The pastor sent an evangelist to conduct Sunday services in our own village. Some people from other villages joined with us, and we now have forty members in our small assembly. We are now planning and believing for a church building. Please pray for us."

A Servant Named Sam

The key that unlocks the door to film evangelism and eventually to church-planting is the film unit leader. I'd like you to meet one of them. His name is Sam.

I met the thirty-year-old man at the hotel where I was staying in India. He picked me up in one of our Dayspring mini-vans.

Sam knew only a few words of English, so it was impossible to do much talking. He just took my bags and drove me to the places I needed to go. That same day he worked on the speakers, repaired the wiring, tested the microphones and loaded the equipment into the van for our journey to a film showing that night. When the road gave out, Sam carried the equipment on his back as we walked the narrow winding paths through the bush to show the film.

117

When we arrived at the clearing, it was Sam who set up the screen, prepared the equipment, wired the temporary light fixtures and turned them on with the generator. He ran the projector during the film showing and prayed with those who came forward for salvation.

After the meeting he took down the equipment, carried it back to the van and packed it neatly, and we began the long ride back home.

Bright and early the next morning it was Sam who picked me up for the ride to the airport. On the way he glanced over his shoulder and said, "I film unit leader" — then went right back to his driving.

Perhaps that is what impressed me most about Sam — how much he was like Jesus. He never did anything to call attention to who he was. All he did was serve — quietly doing everything without recognition. The only thing I heard was that one simple sentence — not proud but pleased — "I film unit leader."

In reality Sam was far more than that. He speaks five native languages and is one of our most dynamic film team leaders, winning thousands of people to the Lord through his powerful preaching and dedication to present *Oceans of Mercy*.

Sam and hundreds of others just like him are giving their lives for a new kind of evangelism — presenting the gospel on the silver screen.

EIGHT

YOU'RE
COMMISSIONED!

Many people consider the Great Commission a mandate of shame: "You'd better do it, or their blood will be dripping from your hands!" It is just one more pressure facing a willing Christian who is worried about learning a second language, hoping God won't send him to Africa or the Amazon and wondering if he'll be living a meager existence and wearing secondhand clothes.

On the day I finally knew Jesus was real, everything changed for me. After that encounter with Jesus in Pat Robertson's office I was filled with joy and love. I couldn't help but tell what I had experienced.

Today I tell young people, "It's easy to get in gear with the great message of the gospel. There is nothing accidental or haphazard about salvation. This is the God who sees ahead and makes provision. He'll empower you, give you resources and supply your needs." Yes, there will be challenges and disappointments, but it will be so exciting and adventurous. It's far beyond going into the Peace Corps or any social program you could join. There's nothing to compare with telling those in "paradise lost" the wonderful news of the Savior.

The most important words of Jesus while He was on earth were those He gave to His disciples just before the ascension: "And He said to them, 'Go into all the world and preach the gospel to every creature' " (Mark 16:15).

Just prior to His death, Christ met with the disciples and told them what was about to happen. But they did not believe He was going to die. "Then Jesus said to them, 'All of you will be made to stumble because of Me this night, for it is written: "I will strike the Shepherd, and the sheep of the flock will be scattered" ' " (Matt. 26:31).

Then Christ said something extraordinary: "But after I have been raised, I will go before you to Galilee" (v. 32). His words were referring to after the crucifixion. "Then the eleven disciples went away into Galilee, to the mountain which Jesus had appointed for them" (Matt. 28:16).

The Lord told them that night in the garden that He was facing a terrible tragedy but that He would meet them in a few days *on the other side of death!* Peter, however, couldn't see that far ahead. He said, "Even if all are made to stumble because of You, I will never be made to stumble" (Matt. 26:33). But Jesus said, "Assuredly, I say to you that this night, before the rooster crows, you will deny Me three times" (v. 34).

The disciples could not comprehend the great thing

that was about to happen. Nevertheless, the Lord informed them even before His trial that He was going to have an appointment with them at a particular location after He was raised. He could have met them in Jerusalem, but instead He met them at the "appointed place" — one hundred miles away. It was on that mountain that Christ gave the disciples the Great Commission. Standing there in resurrection glory, He said, "All authority has been given to Me" (Matt. 28:18), and they could see the Almighty's great design unfolding.

Are you beginning to understand what God's plan is all about? Do you know what it is that God wants to do in your life? Even before the cross, God made an appointment to deliver His greatest message: "Go into all the world and preach the gospel to every creature."

God promises not only to meet us on the other side of every problem, challenge or defeat, but He goes through those trials with us. Why? Because He has a grand purpose for our lives. He has an "appointed place" for us.

The Great Commission is truly great! It is a magnificent plan of redemption for the whole world. Even more, it becomes great to those who allow themselves to be *involved* with Christ's commission.

The moment you begin to follow the Lord's command, you enter into the stream of the heart of God — the same river of love that has been flowing since creation. You're part of His master plan to bring fallen humanity into the glorious light of the gospel — and that is a divine honor.

When David was about to build the temple, the Lord took him to the "design room." The Holy Spirit said to him, "Come up; I'm going to show you the master plan of the temple." The blueprint came directly from God. David didn't create it or labor over its design. (See 1 Chron. 28:11.)

That's how it is with our response to the Great Commission, God's plan. The Holy Spirit works through ordinary vessels — people who come from modest backgrounds, who suffer from inferiority complexes and who often have difficulty in communicating. Don't worry about your deficiencies or handicaps. Instead, examine your objective. You will be surprised at what God can do! Remember, God uses "...the foolish things of the world to confound the wise; and God hath chosen the weak things of the world to confound the things which are mighty" (1 Cor. 1:27, KJV).

Paul considered himself a weak vessel, yet he said, "I have made it my aim to preach the gospel, not where Christ was named, lest I should build on another man's foundation, but as it is written: 'To whom He was not announced, they shall see; and those who have not heard shall understand' " (Rom. 15:20-21).

He spoke with total confidence. "They *shall* see. They *shall* understand." What strong message could change minds and hearts so absolutely?

The apostle was referring to the words of the prophet Isaiah. "So shall He sprinkle many nations. Kings shall shut their mouths at Him; for what had not been told them they shall see, and what they had not heard they shall consider" (Is. 52:15).

The word "sprinkle" means "to startle." Why are the leaders of the nations so taken aback? Because they have just seen the image of a terribly marred Savior who died for them. They are stunned.

Paul's strategy is at the very heart of the Great Commission. His aim was to preach Christ boldly where He is not known until everyone has heard.

Today those "who do not know" include a staggering total of nearly three *billion* people. These are precious souls — alive on planet Earth at this very moment but lost for eternity unless they hear the gospel. The problem is that less than 10 percent of the world's mission force is working among these unreached people.

God has a wonderful will for your life, and He wants you to put it into action. As one minister said, "If it glorifies God, and no one else is doing it effectively — and you are available — then do it."

You may ask, Will those who have never heard truly comprehend? Will they grasp the truth of the redemption story without preparation? Doesn't it take time for someone to be saved? Look again at the Word. They "will understand."

Ven Katuratam was a leper covered from head to toe with oozing sores. He had been a fisherman until the dreaded disease struck. Now he was confined to a room, separated from his dear wife and children, fed like an animal under the door.

One night he managed to sneak out after hearing a loud speaker announcement for the film showing. He had never seen a film before. He slipped along the shadows of the buildings and huts and hid in the darkness watching the story of Jesus. When he saw Jesus heal the leper he couldn't believe his eyes. After the film showing he sought the pastor.

"Can this Jesus help me?" he pleaded desperately. That pastor led Ven Katuratam to Christ that evening. Through prayer and treatment over a period of time the leprosy healed. I have seen his joyful face and the many scars that remain. But Ven Katuratam is happily working again, united with his family, and, most of all, he now wants to be a witness for Jesus to other lepers.

The book of Acts records the amazing results that followed the anointed preaching of Peter. He didn't worry about the outcome; he simply proclaimed the death and resurrection of Jesus. What happened? "Many of those who heard the word believed; and the number of the men came to be about five thousand" (Acts 4:4). They understood.

It's important to understand that the Holy Spirit goes ahead of us to draw people to a place of repentance. Our job is not to bring conviction but to bring the message of the good news.

The new converts that came after Peter's sermon had to have a church. They first met in homes, but the crowds got so big they moved to the temple steps. Peter didn't just preach New Testament doctrine — he demonstrated it. It was happening all around them. They were so hungry for Jesus that they said, "Tell us more!" He told them what he had *seen*. They said, "Tell us about the time you cut off the soldier's ear!" And Peter told them. Years later, John said there was not enough ink or paper to write all that the Lord had done.

They Don't Believe It

On a journey to Israel in 1975 I was standing on perhaps the very steps leading past Caiaphas's house where Peter denied Christ — where he warmed his hands in the fires of the Lord's persecutors. It was in the darkness of early morning. A few lights twinkled in the valley below where Bethlehem lay. My heart was filled with love for the Savior as I imagined Him staggering, whipped and bleeding, down those stone steps.

Suddenly the shrill crow of a lonesome rooster pierced the dawn air. I was hearing what Peter must have heard, and it was an awful signal. It crowed a second time. O Lord, don't let it crow again, I thought. To my dismay — as if to mock me — it crowed again, loud enough for all of Jerusalem to hear. A conviction surged though me as I questioned, Have I denied Christ by being too silent a witness?

To my great relief the cock crowed a fourth time.

If we have seen the Savior, we are also witnesses. Just as a witness testifies in a court of law, we only need to tell what we have seen — not what we think or feel. Aren't you glad you don't have to tell the lost what you *think*? It is what you have *seen* that makes you, like Peter, an effective witness.

How do we expand the work of the Lord? By recruiting new witnesses. Our responsibility is not for the *results* of the gospel. We are only commanded to *proclaim it*.

Amazing things happen when people realize they have been commissioned. It transforms their thoughts, their prayers and their actions.

The need for involvement is urgent. In North America it is estimated that less than 20 percent of the churches have a missions committee. Less than 5 percent have any kind of yearly organized event which emphasizes world evangelism to the entire congregation. The situation borders on rebellion against Christ's command.

Many escape the responsibility by saying, "Oh, we have a missions department in our denomination that takes care of those kinds of things." But the Great Commission was not given to a special agency or force. Nor is it the exclusive domain of a missionary or pastor. If you are a disciple of Jesus and plan to follow Him, you're commissioned! You're authorized to go — summoned to tell what you have seen and to become a witness to His redeeming love. It's not that you have to go — *you get to go*. There's a big difference.

It's exciting to get up every morning knowing the Commander-in-Chief has given you a specific task, a clear plan and abundant resources to see His objective accomplished. God doesn't abandon you in the midst of the battle.

As a young man, missionary evangelist T.L. Osborn

attended a conference at the People's Tabernacle in Toronto where the missionary statesman Oswald J. Smith was pastor. He heard the plea for making the Great Commission the supreme task. Osborn's heart was so stirred that he imagined reaching the lost in ways many had never dreamed of.

That young man went on to conduct giant rallies in Third World countries, print tons of literature daily and support up to twenty thousand native pastors involved in reaching the unreached. Many of those he won to Christ are the backbone of native evangelism today. He was just one man, but he took his commission seriously.

For centuries people have tried to shrug off the command of Christ. William Carey, the eighteenth-century missionary to India and the father of modern mission enterprise, had great difficulty convincing his peers in London that the Great Commission was upon *all* their shoulders. When Carey read his famous speech outlining the duty of the church to make it a priority to reach the millions of unreached of his day, one committee member stated vehemently, "Sit down, young man. If God wanted to reach the heathen, He would do it Himself."

Such phrases still echo today.

Satan and the Closed Lands

Oswald J. Smith's classic *The Challenge of Missions* describes a scene that happened long ago. I have read it many times.

Satan is standing before a number of the princes of various regions of the earth getting a report. He is delighted with the news that missionary efforts by disciples of Christ have been thwarted on many fronts. There is great cheering and joy as the reports come in, especially when the news is confirmed that the Closed Lands have not been penetrated.

One of the princes speaks, "Wilt thou not tell us, oh, thou Mighty One, why thou art so anxious to keep the knowledge [the gospel] from these our empires? Knowest thou not that the kingdoms of the Prince of India, the Prince of China and His Royal Highness the Prince of Africa, are being invaded by strong forces, and that men are turning to Christ every day?"

"Ah, yes, full well I know. But listen all, and I will explain why I'm so jealous for the Closed Lands," Satan answered.

"There are several prophecies, perhaps best summed up in this one," he said, "which reads as follows: 'This gospel of the kingdom shall be preached in all the world for a witness unto all nations; and then shall the end come.' Now it is very clear," he continued in a low tone, "that God is visiting the Gentiles, 'to take out of them a people for His name,' and '*after* this,' He says, 'I will return'; and the Great Commission implies that disciples are to be made from among all nations.

"Now," he said indignantly, "Jesus Christ cannot return to reign until every nation has heard the Good News, for it reads, 'I beheld a great multitude, which no man could number, of all nations, and kindreds, and people, and tongues' (Rev. 7:9). Hence, it matters not how many missionaries are sent to countries already evangelized, nor how many converts are made, for not until the message of the Gospel has been proclaimed in Alaska, Tibet, Afghanistan and our other domains, where it has never yet been heard, will He return to reign."

"Then," the Prince of Nepal interrupted, "if we can keep every messenger out of the Closed Lands, we can prevent His coming to reign on the earth and so frustrate the purposes of the Most High."

"And that we will," shouted the proud Prince of Cam-

127

bodia. "Only the other day a missionary himself wrote saying, 'At this time we do not know of a single Cambodian who has a saving knowledge of our Savior Jesus Christ.' We will see to it, Your Majesty, that not one escapes."

"That is good," replied Satan. "Let us be even more vigilant and frustrate every attempt to enter the Closed Lands."

Smith concluded his story by writing, "As the great plan dawned upon them, they shouted with glee, and hurried back to their empires, more determined than ever to prevent the escape of a single soul" (used by permission of G.R. Welch Company, Limited).

Breaking the Boundaries

Today much has changed. The gospel has touched many people to whom Oswald J. Smith referred. For the first time in history, megaspheres of people including the Muslims, Buddhists, Hindus and tribal groups are reachable.

The challenge, however, is still enormous.

It's not enough merely to set our feet into a country. That may only represent a geographical or political boundary. The Bible talks about reaching "tribes, tongues, and people" as well as nations. In India, for example, there are over three thousand people groups with distinct cultures. We must disciple each one. Mission research tells us there are over twelve thousand different families of nations that have yet to be reached with the gospel. We preach about prosperity yet seem to ignore the fact that there are more than four hundred Scripture references to the poor and oppressed, who are God's priority.

According to Edward R. Dayton in *Unreached Peoples*,

"A people group can be considered 'reached' if there is a body of Christians with the potential to evangelize its own people such that outside, cross-cultural efforts can be 'safely' terminated." We see this clearly underway in a number of areas totally unreached two generations ago.

In India our goal is to win entire families to Christ. We feel it is the best way to reach people like the Hindus who are so caste and clan conscious. Foreign witnesses are generally not the most effective in these situations.

The great importance of indigenous film evangelism is that it eliminates cultural barriers. Many people believe that since our world is now a global village, we can send a video through satellite and drop the message to any point on earth. We fail to realize that even if the unreached become a "receiver," they can rarely relate to the "sender."

The Right Wavelength

As both diplomats and missionaries have learned, advances in technology are light years ahead of our communications skills. We have great methods of sharing information, but we don't seem to know how to say it. Those who have ministered in foreign nations know that it takes more then a good interpreter to get the point across. The message itself must be on the right wavelength.

I believe there is only one effective way to penetrate cultural barriers, and that is through native people of that country. They must interpret the gospel in their own culture, language and experience.

Let me give you an example. When a Westerner says yes, his head nods up and down. But when a person in India says yes, his head pivots from left to right and back again. In *Daya Sagar*, when the disciples are listening to

Jesus and believe what He is saying, their heads swivel in this beautiful motion that is peculiar to the Indian people. The gospel is made clear because it has been contextualized.

It's exciting to see how native Christians have accepted the responsibility for their nations. To watch new pastors being commissioned by their own people at a church conference puts a lump in my throat. You can see their hearts beating for the lost and dying. What's even more thrilling is that they are quite capable of using the means at their disposal in new and innovative ways.

The white face is not going to evangelize this present world which includes three billion lost souls. Certainly there are going to be those who are called to go. But I believe those from Western nations should spend their time discipling the few, not the many. Those involved in missions must provide intensive, ever-increasing training and enabling for nationals who are committed to reaching their people. One native Christian has more impact than a compound full of foreign missionaries.

We are at the point where even cross-cultural evangelism is going to be a thing of the past. The next great wave of missions will be a cultural experience all the way.

You ask, "John, then why are you involved? Aren't you an American?"

Yes. But my contribution is to put the tools of evangelism in the hands of nationals and say, "Go!" Our task is to provide the concepts, materials, resources, fellowship, prayer and encouragement without being paternalistic.

The days of natives being servants to foreign missionaries are buried. It is the national pastor-evangelist-teacher who now must present Christ to his people. Our job is to empower him. Some may argue in particular against giving financial assistance to national leaders — that it spoils them. Then let us stop "spoiling" Christian workers everywhere. No, we must be enablers. Without our help it will take much, much longer to fulfill the Great Commission.

New Leadership

Is film evangelism the only way? No! I believe it is the best way to harvest millions of new converts quickly. But we desperately need libraries, printed materials, teachers, Bible schools and great international Christian colleges and universities. I can see native Christians rising up to fill every post.

Ben Huwalli, for example, is the twenty-three-year-old son of prominent medical surgeons in India. He was raised a Hindu. His life was one of wealth and privilege; his family was close to the ruling Gandhi family. However, when Ben began his studies at the university in Bombay, he became rebellious and was soon the leader of a very rough gang. One day, in his desperation, he went to the library and began to read. The book was the New Testament. He was convicted of his life and the next Sunday went to a Christian church and sat in the back pew. The couple seated next to him invited him to their home, where he accepted the Lord as his Savior.

I recently met Ben. He has graduated from Bible school in America and has finished a master's degree. He's now in the process of establishing a Christian university in Bombay on a million-dollar piece of land that was donated by a Hindu businessman. "John," he said, "we will establish a communications training program that will penetrate the nation with the gospel." Even Ben's parents have found Christ.

That's the kind of leadership God is raising up.

It is rare indeed for a Western missionary to be truly accepted by the people. I love the story of an American who won the hearts of the Kaka tribe on the open grass-lands of eastern Cameroon by eating their food. Someone wrote, "An emptied pan of caterpillars is more convincing than all the empty metaphors of love which missionaries are prone to expend on the heathen."

We must discard the notion that we have a superior way of life to which the world should conform. We haven't been called to *destroy* cultures but to *redeem* them.

When God created Adam and Eve, He told them to cultivate the earth — to explore its vast treasures. He gave them the exciting joy of discovery. Even when they fell, God promised that from their seed a Savior would come to purchase back what had been taken. The world was to be redeemed.

Who Is the Greatest?

I've often been asked, "Who is the true missionary?"

My answer is: any person who accepts the Lord's call to fulfill the commission. There are certainly within that group highly trained and skilled specialists, but there is still a call on every Christian's life to "go." It can be done in many, many ways.

Let me tell you about two brothers who were both raised with the call of God on their lives. One went to China and gave thirty years of his life in missionary service. The other remained home to build a business so that he could support his brother. Who is the greatest?

My own mother spent years on a bed of affliction. All she could do was pray — but her intercession reached around the world.

Your response to God's call will likely be totally different from mine. What is eternally important, however, is that you respond.

You will go through trials. Your vision will be tested.

But your calling will also be confirmed and supported. I was very despondent over leaving Pat Robertson, who was not only a great Christian model for me but also a personal friend. At that time I did not fully comprehend my calling — at least not clearly enough to communicate it properly. But later, when I showed Pat the soul-winning strategy that was working in India, he became my strongest ally and supporter.

What Christ told the disciples after the resurrection at that "appointed place" on the mountain, He meant for you and me. He wasn't giving them a choice; He was giving a command.

You're commissioned!

NINE

BREAKING
THE BARRIERS

How do we make the gospel culturally relevant? That question has always been a great challenge for the church.

From the time Hudson Taylor was five years old, he had a vision of reaching China for the Lord. It burned within him. He could think of nothing else but God's love and His compassion for the multiplied millions who lived in the villages of that great country.

Taylor, however, was subjected to the misunderstandings and ridicule of other missionaries in China because of his honest attempts to understand Chinese culture. He wanted to know everything possible about the people he loved so deeply.

The other missionaries were skeptical — even ignorant — of his reasons for wearing the Chinese garb and cutting his hair in the Chinese fashion. But the Holy Spirit was guiding Hudson Taylor, showing him how important it is to understand the people the Lord sends you to reach.

Taylor's wife became seriously ill, and they returned to Brighton Beach, England, where he spent time praying and contemplating how to reach inland China. As he walked along the seaside, he prayed for just twenty-four workers to help him in this effort. But God enlarged his vision, and Taylor eventually established China Inland Mission. More than six thousand workers joined him to establish a church that has remained vibrant and strong through great persecution. Much of what is happening in China today is a result of Taylor's heartbeat for the people.

Hopping Fences

In trying to reach a nation, the cultural hurdles faced by outsiders are so great that they make the Great Wall of China seem two inches high.

Most Westerners believe that once we have bridged the gap between two major cultures, our task is complete. But the walls that separate people *within* major regions are much greater than we realize. For example, an all-Chinese version of the story of Jesus would not be readily accepted in Japan. The same is true of Korea — they see themselves as totally unique and would be critical of an all-Japanese version.

Spreading the gospel from culture to culture is not like hopping fences. The barriers are formidable, and it does not happen spontaneously. The racial and class discrimination we know in the West is minor compared to that experienced by most Third World people. As a result it is extremely difficult for one tribe or ethnic group to spread Christ's message to another — they generally won't receive it.

Many native languages have a word to describe the native people as "human beings" but no such word to describe outsiders. It's as if others do not truly exist.

We are guilty too. Modern man has for centuries made a great distinction between "chosen people" and dangerous aliens. In the church we have drawn a line between true believers and the "heathen." Until the last few years there have been almost no common meeting points. It seemed that the concepts or values of one group were not valid in the other. Unfortunately, many of those barriers still remain.

If we are to fulfill the Great Commission, we must realize that all people are God's creation. The heart of a tribal warrior from New Guinea beats just the same as a member of the House of Lords in London. Their blood is the same color, and their bodies function in the exact same ways. The differences are not biological; they are in culture and environment.

An Oriental child adopted by an occidental couple learns English, embraces the attitudes of children he plays with and chooses a professional life just as his classmates do.

That same process happens on a broader scale when a group of people chooses new values and customs of behavior. There are some villages in South India where the entire population has been converted to Christ, and now they base their lives on the teaching of Scripture. As a result of their belief, their behavior has been changed drastically. They are worlds apart from a village steeped in Hinduism in the foothills of the Himalayas.

Stranger in Samaria

The cultural walls that must be broken to reach people with the gospel are more than simply a difference in language. Prejudice runs deep. Rivalries between neighboring nations — such as Arabs versus Jews in the Middle East — are real. Social values are often as different as night and day. My missionary friend Don Richardson discovered in one tribe that the highest virtue was treachery. Judas became their hero until Don found a way to communicate the truth of Jesus' love. That's why the most effective way to reach a Malaysian is from the message of a Malaysian. As audiences in India gaze at the film telling the story of Jesus, they think, This must be true. These are our people telling the story. Every culture tends to favor its own.

The Lausanne Committee for World Evangelization, speaking about reaching the Chinese, said in *Proclaim Christ Until He Comes: Lausanne II in Manila*: "We believe we stand today on the threshold of the greatest ingathering in Christ of the Chinese people this world has ever known. But, more, our larger concern is that in these last days God will transform the Chinese church into a missionary vehicle through which the Christian gospel will be brought to the forgotten and hidden peoples of this generation."

Jesus overcame cross-cultural barriers creatively. Traveling through Samaria, He and the disciples stopped at Jacob's well, and the Lord spoke to a woman who came to draw water. "Jesus said to her, 'Give Me a drink.' For His disciples had gone away into the city to buy food. Then the woman of Samaria said to Him, 'How is it that You, being a Jew, ask a drink from me, a Samaritan woman?' " (John 4:7-9).

Tremendous racial discrimination and hatred existed

between Jews and Samaritans — and for a Jewish man to be speaking to a local woman was even more astonishing. But the Lord did not allow that to hinder Him. He used those circumstances to communicate with great sensitivity. "Jesus answered and said to her, 'If you knew the gift of God, and who it is who says to you, "Give Me a drink," you would have asked Him, and He would have given you living water' " (v. 10).

Using the well, a physical symbol of the message He came to deliver, Jesus said to her, "Whoever drinks of this water will thirst again, but whoever drinks of the water that I shall give him will never thirst. But the water that I shall give him will become in him a fountain of water springing up into everlasting life" (vv. 13-14).

The response to the message and to her witness was great. "Come, see a Man who told me all things..." (v. 29). The Lord had to delay His journey to Galilee for two days because so many people crowded around Him and "believed" (v. 41).

There are many, many Samarias in our world. We call them "people groups," and most research places the number at about seventeen thousand. Of those, only five thousand are considered to have a viable church.

Recently I heard a Christian broadcaster say, "Through shortwave radio we are now reaching the entire world for Christ." It sounds exciting until we realize that nearly three billion people have yet to hear the gospel. Have we reached a nation or tribe just because one person has heard? Or because an electronic signal falls from the sky on a remote population with just a few receivers? I believe the mandate of Christ includes establishing a body of believers among each group, as one of our teams did among a tribe called the Gaddis — a group of eighty thousand shepherd people living high in the Himalayas.

Specifically, the great challenges we face are the 235

million unreached Buddhists in the Far East, the billion-plus people of China, the Hindu world population of over 900 million, the same approximate number of Muslims, plus over 200 million in thousands of tribal groups scattered around the globe. It's a herculean task.

The Golden Message

Over the centuries, each nation or tribe has developed a unique value system. That's why it is important that the gospel be communicated to each people group in a distinctive, culturally relevant manner.

Most Americans have no comprehension of what it takes to communicate the gospel in a foreign land. It's like a Wall Street banker trying to build a church in a ghetto of Atlanta — multiplied one thousand times.

Recently I listened in horror as an American evangelist preached a prosperity message to a native Indian audience of five or six thousand people who didn't have two rupees — about eleven cents — to get rice for lunch.

"Christians are afraid of money," he said. "God has paved the streets with purest gold, but we're afraid to have gold in our pockets or rings on our hands. He wants us to have the finest clothes."

I was incensed. I wanted to run up to him and say, Brother, what right do you have to come to this village? You've never walked in their shoes; you've never participated in their life-style. How long do you think it's going to take to change the economy of India to get to a place where they can prosper as you are talking about?

The message he brought may have been relevant in Dallas, but not in Delhi.

My Indian companion leaned over and said, "Don't worry. The interpreter is not preaching this American's sermon. He is giving the people a more practical message."

We can't export "American" Christianity. Scripture is Scripture, but how we apply it is based on our environment and personal experience. We should never change the heart of the gospel, but we must make it applicable to the people we are trying to reach.

The word communication means "commonness." Paul wrote about it when he said, "For though I am free from all men, I have made myself a servant to all, that I might win the more; and to the Jews I became as a Jew, that I might win Jews; to those who are under the law, as under the law, that I might win those who are under the law; to those who are without law, as without law (not being without law toward God, but under law toward Christ), that I might win those who are without law; to the weak I became as weak, that I might win the weak. I have become all things to all men, that I might by all means save some" (1 Cor. 9:19-22).

It is only when we find common ground with people we want to reach that the message gets through. Otherwise they are only hearing noise, and *we* become the message instead of the Word of the Lord. God forbid.

Many unreached people are finally made to see the gospel through analogies in their own culture. Don Richardson, author of *Eternity in Their Hearts*, explains that a key to "contextualizing" the gospel is found in "concept fulfillment." How can we talk about our hearts being cleansed whiter than snow when the people we are trying to reach have never seen snow? If we change the words to "whiter than the sand of the sea," are we changing the message? I don't believe we are.

God's Culture

Many Americans equate being different as being backward or uncivilized. As you travel the world you soon realize that every culture has its virtues and its vices.

The power of the gospel speaks directly to evil regardless of where it is found. It may be cannibalism, widow burning, infanticide, tribal warfare — or abortion, homosexuality, greedy capitalism or godless communism.

Just as every culture has its dark side, it also has its beauty and worth. We must see it as God's culture, which He wants to redeem through His Son. Richardson points out that in the heart of every man there is a vacuum waiting to be filled with the message of redemption. When that happens, society conforms to God's standards whether it be in the jungle, the desert, the mountains or the city.

The work of translating or "transposing" the gospel to the nations of the world has been underway for centuries. Great Christian missionaries of every church and practice of faith have laid the foundation. They have sown seed in soil so rocky that it needed to be plowed again and again before there was even the smallest harvest.

Noble men and women have prayed untold hours and have even sacrificed their lives for the sake of Christ — it's been said that their blood and tears have "softened the soil." Without question God will greatly reward their efforts. The time has come, however, for us to face reality. Individual missionaries must continue to answer God's call, but their numbers are not enough. The problem is too immense, and the gap is widening.

Hinduism is the fastest-growing religion in the world. When I share that fact, people ask, "What's their secret? How are they winning converts?"

"There's no secret, and it's not because of Hindu evangelism," I tell them. "It's simply because of their exploding population."

Recent statistics show that America has only 55,000 missionaries of all kinds and only 10 percent of those are working among unreached people. It is estimated that it would take over 200,000 missionaries to complete the Great Commission. Plus, the number of career people on the mission field is decreasing. But, as *Daya Sagar* demonstrates, there is an answer — and it is working.

Windows of the Soul

Christ was serious about preaching the gospel to all nations, but He left the implementation to us. I believe indigenous film evangelism is the most effective tool we have for reaching India and the Third World with the message. To me it seems evident that God has given the concept for this very purpose.

After seeing *Oceans of Mercy* for the first time, a veteran missionary said, "The crucifixion and resurrection scenes contained more gospel than twenty-five missionaries could present preaching around the clock for a week."

It has been said that the eyes are the windows of the soul. That is why allowing people to "see" the message of the cross has such a life-transforming impact. The key is visualization.

At the age of sixteen, Albert Einstein became preoccupied with the concept of light. He saw a beam of light traveling through infinite space and envisioned himself riding on it. It was out of that experience that he developed his theory of relativity.

What if we could approach the mission challenge as Einstein approached the questions of space, time and matter? What if we could allow our God-given intellect to create answers to the challenge of world missions? The Bible says that "we have the mind of Christ" (1 Cor. 2:16). If we tap into the Lord's source of knowledge and creativity, the unreached people of the world will be touched in ways never before envisioned.

Over the years I have developed a great respect for the villagers. They may not be able to read, but they have enormous intelligence. They don't know anything about the history of the world or about the Berlin Wall, Tiananmen Square, the Gulf War or the new world order, but they have an immense capacity to know God. What did Jesus do when He wanted to tell them, "God loves you, He forgives you and He wants you to have everlasting life"? He went to the cross. God could have planned other ways to save us, but I believe the reason Jesus died on Calvary is because we are a visually oriented people.

Think for a moment about the symbols of redemption in the Old Testament — the sacrifices, the tabernacle in the wilderness and Solomon's temple. God was panto-miming the salvation story. We can picture the bullock being lifted up on the altar. He's moving and alive as he's tied and his throat is slit. The blood spurts out and is sprayed on the garments of the priest. As the people watch, God is saying, "This is the horror of sin. It is being dealt with here." The gospel is visual.

Can They See It?

Why have so many missionaries misfired in their attempts to communicate Christ? We have failed to grasp what Jesus meant when He said, "Go, proclaim." The root word means "make plain — make it understandable." We have not completed the mission until we tell the story in such a way that they can understand.

My objective is to have the villager look upon the screen and digest more gospel in two and a half hours than he could get in a year of preaching or teaching. And it is happening. Consider this testimony from a former Hindu.

I was born into an orthodox Hindu family. My husband is a fruit merchant, and we would travel many towns and bring home all kinds of Hindu pictures and idols to keep our home safe from evil spirits. To us God was a god of wealth. We lived in constant fear that if we did not offer many sacrifices to the gods, we would be killed. We wanted peace, but life was miserable.

When the film *Daya Sagar* was shown in our village, we went to see it. I did not want to think of it any more than a story about a good man. But that night I could not sleep. I kept thinking about Jesus and what the film said He did for me. I had many questions. The next day, without telling anyone, even my husband, I went to see the Christian pastor in our village. As I told him what I was feeling, I began to cry — it was as though something inside of me was turning around. The pastor prayed for me, and I accepted Jesus Christ as my Lord and Savior that day. That night I told my husband, and later he too received Jesus into his heart. Our lives have never been the same. We crushed our idols and burned our pictures of Hindu gods. We have joined the church in our village and have been baptized. Thank you for bringing happiness to our lives. God bless you.

When John had his great revelation on the Isle of Patmos, it was visual. He said, "Then I turned to see the voice that spoke with me..." (Rev. 1:12). What he saw was a description of Jesus — "One like the Son of Man..." (v. 13). "He had in His right hand seven stars, out of His mouth went a sharp two-edged sword, and His countenance was like the sun shining in its strength" (v. 16). What John beheld was so incredible he couldn't fully describe it.

The church has been hearing the voice for two thousand years but has not been able to communicate effectively what it has heard. Today God is saying to the church, "Turn and see the voice. See the One you represent."

The revelation of God is primarily visual. Almost everything God has given us from Genesis to Revelation is described in a visual theme. The Ten Commandments were delivered on tablets that people could see. Moses built a tabernacle that was filled with symbolic meaning — from the brazen altar to the holy of holies. In the temple the veil was torn in two as a visual symbol. At Pentecost the Holy Spirit descended as tongues of fire. Jesus came so that the Word could be "made flesh." That is how Paul saw Christ on the road to Damascus.

Reading God's Word is something we cherish, but there always will be the still, small voice that tells us to *look*. Jesus said, "Do you not say, 'There are still four months and then comes the harvest'? Behold, I say to you, lift up your eyes and look at the fields [see what God sees], for they are already white for harvest!" (John 4:35).

How do you choose the best method of presenting the Lord? Communicating the gospel is both simple and complex. Many would consider it simple, but as Norman Geisler pointed out in *Theology and Mission*, there are "many views of 'Christ,' many ways to 'communicate,' and there are many 'worlds' to which Christ must be communicated."

Language barriers are often the greatest hurdles we must cross when presenting Christ in a foreign land. They are largely overcome, however, when we use a visual approach. That's what sets film evangelism apart from other methods of communicating the gospel.

Every day 60 million people are going to movies somewhere in the world. In India 76 million people go to movies at least once a month. Why? Because people are visual. Television is great — over 750 million sets have been sold, but 460 million of those sets are in North America, Western Europe and Japan. We must understand that the Third World still does not have television — only a few million sets sprinkled among nearly three billion people! (And rarely is a Christian program allowed.) As for radio, less than 5 percent of India owns a set. There are 3.5 billion people in the world without radio or TV!

In our effort to penetrate every nation with the gospel, we must use every means possible. Film isn't the only way, but I believe it is the most effective — and the most overlooked — means of mass evangelism.

More Than Words

The church has centered its focus on the written Word. In the process we have virtually abandoned visual experience as if it were sinful. We've left the "pictures" to Hollywood — who has used them to destroy a generation — while Christians have reluctantly done little with film or dramatic production. To put it another way, the commercial film industry has succeeded in making the unreal seem real while Christians have made the real seem unreal!

Today's cutting-edge missions leaders realize that using the visual medium effectively is fundamental to the success of fulfilling the Great Commission. We can communicate a wider range of emotions and persuasion in a few seconds of video or film than we can in a lengthy sermon.

Imagine two hours and forty-seven minutes of the life

of Jesus already burned into the minds of the villagers. Vicarious suffering is a difficult thing to talk about in words, but they understand it through film. When Barabbas runs up Calvary's hill to Jesus, he sees that Jesus has already died in his place. He cries out "Lord!" — and he is weeping. The audience is keenly aware that Jesus has taken Barabbas's place.

The villagers know from watching the film that Jesus is innocent of the charges brought against Him. The teaching that follows becomes effective because everything has been brought to life. They are ready to receive instruction on *why* His shed blood has the power to redeem them.

I look at our ministry as much more than bringing people to the Lord. At every showing, 10 to 15 percent of the people in the audience respond by saying yes to the gospel. Our biggest challenge is to plant churches and help to disciple them. As one evangelist told me, "I can't wait to preach where you've shown the film. You are cultivating the field for a great harvest."

Without question, indigenous film evangelism has to be one of the shortest routes to planting a church in a targeted population. Why add any unnecessary steps? It is simple, it works, and new converts are often baptized the very next day.

An Indian Christ dying on the cross has resulted in an unprecedented number of people finding salvation. But what about a Spanish Christ for Bolivia? A Korean Christ for Seoul? And, as we'll discuss later, how should we respond to the requests for a black Christ on film in Africa?

TEN

ANSWERING THE CALL

I was attending the annual missions conference of a large denomination at its headquarters. The organization has one of the most aggressive missionary forces in the world. The speakers were electrifying and were filled with a fervor to win the lost at any cost.

Every participant was handed a beautiful full-color report — the kind you would expect from a multinational corporation like IBM. I opened it to see wonderful accounts of progress throughout the world regarding missions appropriations and spending.

When I read the section regarding future goals and

objectives, I was thrilled beyond words. There it was in print: "One of our goals is to bring the gospel during the next year to the sixteen million Tamil-speaking people in India." Since *Oceans of Mercy* is also in that language, I couldn't wait to talk with some of their missions leaders.

"Tell me," I asked, "what kind of strategy are you going to use to reach the Tamils?"

"We're not sure at this point" was the reply. "But we have some missionaries who are committed to go." Their goal seemed to be a dream — a vague hope that it would happen. But they didn't know just how to execute the objective that was on paper.

Later that day I shared my emotions with three of the denominational leaders. "Gentlemen, I feel like a man with the secret formula for Coca-Cola, and no one wants to listen. You've announced a wonderful goal to reach the Tamils, but there's no mention of a plan to do it!"

They listened politely. "I'm frustrated because the tool we need is in our hands. If you will mobilize one hundred native teams to show the film twelve times each month for ten months, to an average audience of 1,350, you can reach the entire sixteen million Tamils in less than a year." Then I added, "What does it cost to field one hundred brand-new teams in India? Probably ten cents per soul reached."

I couldn't understand their apathy. Were they not listening? Had bureaucracy buried new ideas? Were they trapped by tradition? Were they afraid of competition?

Founding Father Syndrome

Why have we failed to establish the church in over twelve thousand unreached people groups? Where is the problem? What is the answer?

The conclusion I've reached is that there is a great

resistance to change among those involved in the leadership of world missions. It's much more than a lack of imagination or creativity. There is not a willingness to risk new methods of evangelism.

The church suffers from what business writer Peter Drucker called "the founding father syndrome." He was referring to the large corporation still headed by a founder who would not relinquish control — often killing the company, or at least keeping it from defeating the competition.

After hundreds of years of missionary effort, nearly three billion have never been reached with the gospel. What is the explanation? David Barrett tackled that question in his book *Evangelize! A Historical Survey of the Concept from B.C. 400 to 1987 A.D.* He gave four primary reasons for the failure of past plans to fulfill the Great Commission:

1) The absence of any clear idea of what it means to reach every person.

2) The absence of an all-embracing global strategy.

3) The absence of the ability to match needs with resources.

4) The absence of any serious attempt to grapple with the logistics required.

Mission outreaches for the most part have been built on the Moses model — let the people come to you. A church in Nebraska sends the money to build a small church in a village of Nigeria. The doors are opened, and people are expected to come and be converted.

Our strategy at Dayspring is exactly the opposite. We are taking the gospel directly to the masses. Right now we have enough requests to put films into the hands of ten thousand native evangelists. God prepares these men for ministry, and our job is to equip them for service. The story of Samuel, one of our most well-known film leaders, is a case in point.

Samuel was nothing but a rickshaw puller, a job so low on India's social scale that men like him are not even tipped by their riders.

He was illiterate, never having learned to read, never being given the opportunity. At night the rickshaw was his bed for he had nowhere else to sleep, spending what little he earned on tobacco and alcohol.

An elderly lady called for Samuel's rickshaw service. Her husband was ill, and she needed to bring him home. Samuel was angry that he had to put a sick man in his rickshaw — it was an insult, even to the low caste — and as he pulled them he treated the old woman rudely. But he was surprised to find her treating him kindly.

When they arrived at the woman's house, she invited Samuel inside. He was shocked, but he agreed. Inside she showed the rickshaw puller a picture of Jesus on the cross. She told him the gospel story — and there in her tiny living room she led Samuel to the Lord.

Samuel fell in love with Jesus, and his heart quickly grew hungry for more of God. A few nights later, as Samuel slept in his rickshaw, he had an amazing dream: The illiterate rickshaw puller dreamed he was able to read — he could read the words "Holy Bible" on the cover of a book and the first verses of Ezekiel 2 inside!

Samuel claimed that vision by faith and began to believe that he would be given the gift of reading — miraculously. He had started attending a local church. One day shortly thereafter Samuel arrived at the church to run an errand, and there he saw a Bible lying on a table.

In a surge of faith he opened it to Ezekiel chapter 2, and he began to read. God had performed a true miracle! To this day Samuel reads perfectly.

Full of the Spirit of God, Samuel began to preach, and under a rich anointing he was soon being used of God in miracles of healing and attracting crowds of up to twenty thousand people. The national press has carried many of the stories. They call Samuel "the God man." Today, every time he speaks, Samuel holds up a simple picture of Jesus, much like the one the woman had used to lead him to the Lord. He carries that picture, tattered and faded, everywhere he goes.

When I visited with Samuel, again and again he asked me to provide a print of *Daya Sagar*. I'll never forget when he showed me the tattered picture of Christ on the cross that he still carries.

"Please give," he stuttered in his broken English, pointing helplessly to the picture of Jesus. Finally, nearly weeping, he begged me to make a copy of the film available.

Samuel had seen firsthand the impact of our ministry — and he wanted to become a part of it. He was asking for an even more effective "picture" of Jesus, for that's what our film really is — a moving photograph of some 280,000 frames that dramatically and effectively presents the love and power of the Lord Jesus Christ.

Those who teach missions have closely examined the methods used to reach the world. Jonathan Lewis discusses four specifics in *World Mission: An Analysis of the World Christian Movement*:

1) The "Standard Solution Strategy." This method is based on working out a particular way of doing things, then uses this same approach in every situation. The problem, however, is a lack of flexibility and failure to take account of what others are doing.

2) The "Being-in-the-Way Strategy." The implication of this approach is that long-range planning is not very important because this is God's job. It is assumed the Lord will lead. "I being in the way, the Lord led me to the house of my master's brethren" (Gen. 24:27, KJV).

3) The "Plan-So-Far Strategy." This tactic assumes that if we devise the plan to *start* the work, God will do the rest. It doesn't focus on outcomes, but beginnings.

4) The "Unique Solution Strategy" assumes that every situation we face is different, and each requires its own answer. Those involved in this method of ministry wait anxiously to see how God is going to inspire people to meet the challenge.

Of these four views, most people involved in missions believe the "Unique Solution Strategy" is the best approach to world evangelism.

Robert Coleman said in *The Master Plan of Evangelism,* "Merely because we are busy, or even skilled doing something does not necessarily mean that we are getting anything accomplished."

My respected friend K.P. Yohannan, founder of Gospel for Asia, is winning thousands of souls through the mobilization of itinerant native evangelists. After seeing the power of *Daya Sagar*, he wrote in a letter to his supporters, "All our mission leaders report that this film is the single most effective tool they have to gain entrance into villages, schools and communities that otherwise would never allow any kind of gospel work."

Yohannan added, "After much prayer we have decided to trust the Lord for one hundred additional films this year. They will be used in India, Nepal, Sri Lanka and other Asian countries."

New Boundaries

Throughout the history of fulfilling the Great Commission, many lessons have been learned the hard way. It took many years, for example, for denominations to come to the conclusion that experienced missionaries on the field were fully capable of formulating plans and policies.

Relationships with other mission boards and church groups also had to be examined. Fortunately, denominations realized that their theological differences preached "back home" were insignificant when faced with winning a new soul to Christ in Africa, India or Asia. One of the results of that conclusion has been "denominationalism by geography." Without entering into each other's turf, each group seeks to evangelize with the least possible duplication of effort. In many nations the Baptists have one territory, the Presbyterians have another, and the Assemblies of God are working in the next.

With the task so overwhelming — and the world shrinking — time-honored methods of world outreach are now being questioned.

Today is a unique time in the history of the church. It's almost a repeat of the times of Christ. In the first century, Rome brought the world together through commerce and military power. Now we are being drawn together by communications technology, diplomatic initiatives, international conglomerates.

I believe the cycle is not accidental but rather a fulfilling of God's Word: "That in the dispensation of the fullness of the times He might gather together in one all things in Christ, both which are in heaven and which are on earth" (Eph. 1:10).

The advance of the gospel has been quickened by man's discoveries. First it was the printing press, then the steam engine, now mass media communications — including television and motion pictures. Technology has brought the world together as never before. In less than thirty-six hours we can physically reach virtually any village in the world.

It's thrilling to know that God's end-time calendar is quickly approaching. When is the midnight hour? Jesus, speaking to His disciples on the Mount of Olives, said,

"And this gospel of the kingdom will be preached in all the world as a witness to all the nations, and then the end will come" (Matt. 24:14).

The boundaries of time have been marked far more clearly than the boundaries of geography. When there has been an effective witness to all the nations or people groups, the Lord will return, but He alone knows that hour. Today we are seeing unprecedented cooperation and networking among mission agencies to see the prophecy fulfilled.

Four Vital Ingredients

In his book *Stop the World, I Want to Get On*, Peter Wagner of Fuller Theological Seminary says there are four vital ingredients for a healthy missions program: the right goals, the right place at the right time, the right methods and the right people.

He believes that making disciples should be the major objective. "Just to know how many attended an evangelistic crusade or how many signed decision cards is helpful, but inadequate. The Lord of the Great Commission, in the final analysis, is interested in disciples, not simply decisions."

Since the founding of Dayspring International our goal has been much more than seeing millions of people won to Christ. We must present the gospel in such a way as to make disciples and to establish healthy, vibrant, self-reproducing local churches in the villages.

He believes that a great missions plan should have three characteristics: biblical, efficient and relevant. "Missions is such a fast-moving field that strategy useful five years ago might well be obsolete today. It needs constant updating."

Within a decade the computer chip has risen to challenge the power of oil in the world's economy. It's been said that Japan could cripple the United States if it refused to sell us those little "brains" made of silicon. Soon the memory of two thousand desktop computers will be stored in a chip the size of a sugar cube. That's forty-four million pages! Now we need to examine how the computer chip can play a major role in bringing in the harvest. Innovators are essential now as never before.

We Need Catalysts

I firmly believe the time for a bold new world missions approach has arrived. The number of professing Christians in the world has *tripled* since 1900, but the percentage of Christians in the world population actually declined during the past fifteen years to 33 percent. It is doubtful that of the 500 million so-called world Christians — those who supposedly understand the Great Commission or at least appreciate its importance — 250 million really desire its fulfillment enough to pray, give and go. In a day when many Christians want a religious experience that "makes them feel good," it is probably more realistic to accept the notion that 20 percent or less will do the real work.

Ross Rhoads recently said to his thirty-five-hundred-member Calvary Church in Charlotte, North Carolina: "The average Christian leads a boring, self-centered, no-thinking and basically fruitless life." He called on the church to arise from its slumber to meet the challenge.

The day of thinking in terms of winning dozens, hundreds or even thousands to Christ must be re-evaluated. Each soul is precious in God's sight, but our methods must include winning *millions* before Christ returns. Hundreds of thousands of churches must be established to accommodate the massive waves of new converts I believe are coming. As Jim Montgomery, founder of DAWN (Discipling A Whole Nation) emphasized, seven million vital congregations presently exist, but that number needs to double as we seek to fulfill the Lord's command.

Dayspring International is but one of hundreds of mission organizations in the world. We cannot do everything. But *what we can do*, we *ought to do*, and by the grace of God *we will do!* Together we must complete the task God has placed before us. Recently I heard the famous German evangelist to Africa, Reinhard Bonnke, speaking on the subject of world harvest. Bonnke last year preached to over five million Africans face-to-face. As many as 500,000 were in a single service. Yet he made this observation to us gathered. "If I preached to a million people a day for the next ten years, still half the world would not have heard the gospel." Bonnke then emphatically exhorted, "The day of the individual evangelist doing the job is over. I have no competitors in soul-winning, only colleagues. The church is a ship on the ocean; lost sinners are sinking everywhere. We need all hands on deck in this business of rescuing the lost. There must be other ways besides mass crusades."

We cannot afford to take a moment of rest when we see how the world's religions have dedicated themselves to their own version of foreign missions. America now has a $25-million Buddhist temple in Los Angeles, a Hindu temple — one of the world's largest — in Chicago and an Islamic Center for Evangelism in New York. Saudi Arabia recently gave $50 million to spread the message of Islam in America.

When it comes to global missions, I believe that foreign missionaries should assume the role of a catalyst.

In chemistry it takes only small quantities of a catalyst to have a powerful effect on the reacting substance —

sometimes only a few parts per million. The word comes from the Greek word *kataleuin*, which means "to break down" (*kata*) and "to set free" (*leuin*).

Again and again the Lord has asked me, "Do you want to make a difference?"

"Yes, Lord," I have answered. "By Your grace I will."

God expects His people to bring about change. Listen to the final words of Jesus to His disciples on the Mount of Olives: "But you shall receive power when the Holy Spirit has come upon you; and you shall be witnesses to Me in Jerusalem, and in all Judea and Samaria, and to the end of the earth" (Acts 1:8).

The moment you become a witness you become an agent for uniting sinners with the Lord. Paul said, "Now all things are of God, who has reconciled us to Himself through Jesus Christ, and has given us the ministry of reconciliation" (2 Cor. 5:18). Is there anything greater?

What does a witness tell? He shares what he has *seen*, and the Holy Spirit gives the testimony its power! When a true Christian comes in contact with the lost world, there is a spiritual effect as mighty as the chemical reaction of nitroglycerin set off. As they said of Paul and Silas, "These who have turned the world upside down have come here too" (Acts 17:6).

You'll never know the power of your witness until you activate it. That's why the Lord said, "Go!" He wants us to demonstrate the good news. Many people, however, seem to be clothed in a protective wrapper — just in case someone may be impacted by their lives. They are afraid of the results. It's time to be poured out, not bottled up.

A true catalyst sows the seed and allows God to be glorified by the abundant harvest. In other words, don't make yourself the issue. Too often great moves of God have been ruined because men and women who were used mightily decided to claim what was not theirs. It's disturbing to see people who direct souls to Calvary suddenly turn the attention to themselves, causing their followers to believe in them more than in the God of whom they testified. Nothing made this truth clearer to me than when I was present for a showing of *Daya Sagar* in one of the largest slums in all of Asia.

In this slum, where five million people huddle together in absolute poverty beneath scraps of tin, bits of broken shingles and strips of plastic and cardboard, where rodents of unexplainable filth play with tiny children, we set up our large white movie screen. It hung high across an alley between two rickety buildings. Four alleyways converged deep inside these slums and emptied into a small square that would later hold a crowd of several thousand.

Facing the small square was one of the few churches for these masses. Inside was the cleanest spot in the slums, the church tile floor. Attached to the side of the church building in one of the alleys it faced was a lean-to shed about five feet high containing a pile of greasy black cooking coal. A single forty-watt bulb dangled by a naked cord. As I contemplated the striking scene, the pastor approached me asking how he should introduce me before the film showing.

"Pastor," I began, "this is your place; these are your people. Thank you for thinking of me, but I have not come to be introduced. You must take the microphone and welcome these people. Tell them the true and living God has enabled you to bring the story of His Son. After the film, lead them to Christ and tell them you will teach them more about this wonderful Jesus. I must stay out of sight. They must not see my white face. So I will just sit in that coal bin and pray for them and for you, that God will bless you."

It is vital that in our search for the one important task

God has called us to do, we stay hidden behind the cross. A true catalyst understands the source of his power.

Greater Goals

I came out of CBN with such an enormous palette of ideas that it was hard for me to know which ones I should delete from the list. Eventually I narrowed the ideas from twenty, to three or four, and finally to only one. It wasn't until I locked in on indigenous film evangelism that miracles of ministry began to happen.

God has a unique place of service for every Christian. For me this was it! There was a great job to do, and I did not care who received the credit.

Dayspring's philosophy is to team up with others who share the burden for global evangelism. As I recently told a missions conference, "We truly do not seek ownership or control. We want to be an enabling servant to the native evangelist, pastor and teacher and to network with anyone who has a world vision."

When Ernest Komanapalli began to share my burden for film evangelism in India, he already had a successful program of training native pastors and establishing churches. His original objective was to establish five hundred congregations as a direct result of our strategy. That number has already been surpassed. "John," he told me recently, "our new goal is to build one thousand churches, and even more."

With only one hundred Christian leaders like Ernest who have a burning desire and a willingness to work, 100,000 churches could be planted in India as a result of *Oceans of Mercy*. That army of leaders is now being commissioned.

There is a great difference, however, between "setting up" churches and planting churches. I like to think of a planted church as having roots of its own — to draw nourishment, produce fruit and continue the cycle of feeding a hungry world.

There is nothing more exhilarating than to see an entire churchful of new converts. Because they've been won to Christ quickly, they believe that others will respond in the same way. Perhaps that is why we are seeing the numbers multiply so rapidly. Within a very short time these new converts are grounded in the Word and are able to evangelize neighboring villages, plant new churches, teach them to become church-planters and so forth. This is why our master plan includes seeing tens of thousands of new churches taking root in India and elsewhere within the next few years. K.P. Yohannan told me on the phone one day, "John, I now truly believe all of India can be reached."

I am thrilled when I see a convert from a previously unreached people group start winning his relatives and friends to the Lord and assemble them into Christian fellowship.

Recently in the tiny Hindu village of Randu, Bihar, a sixteen-year-old girl came to know Jesus as her Savior through *Daya Sagar*, reported team leader N.J. Vargese. This young lady became so excited about her discovery that she ran home immediately and told her family and friends: She had met the true Messiah!

Two of her friends then became so happy about the good news that they received Christ as their Lord and Savior, too — all because of her witness! But that isn't the end to this beautiful story. These two girls later went out and told their friends about what had happened, and eight more people received Christ as their Savior and Lord.

This was just like Andrew running to his brother Peter and telling him about Jesus, but it was in the twentieth century. We have no way of knowing how many hundreds of thousands of times this has happened through our life-of-Christ film.

Gathering a great harvest is only the first step of our mission. That's why we are linking our film ministry with fellowships, denominations and native evangelism efforts which are called to train pastors and build churches.

Recent world events should not detour our global efforts. Since the time of Christ, the church has advanced most dramatically during periods of great social, economic and political unrest.

The Essential Ingredient

Strategies are necessary, but *revival* is the one element that is indispensable before launching an all-out offensive. If God's anointing and power do not accompany our efforts, they will be a waste of time and toil. He has already given the call to arms, but we must move in His might and strength.

We must understand that *true revival always results in the salvation of lost souls and a spontaneous wave of evangelistic effort.* The acid test of revival movements is always the same: the supernatural presence of the Lord in the midst of His people.

In our own nation revival has touched down like a mighty whirlwind, only to rise again and descend in another place. But the outpourings of God's Spirit have given absolute proof that revival produces unprecedented soul-winning.

I've been asked, "Will revival cure the ills of the Third World?" It's a fair question, and one that is answered by the facts of history. Revival not only produces spiritual awakening but major social reform as well. In nineteenth-century England, for example, the Salvation Army launched a plan to expose child slavery, and the repercussions were felt worldwide. A strong spirit of revival accompanied their efforts. The movement was so strong it influenced the feelings of Americans about slavery and helped put Abraham Lincoln into the presidency. Slavery was then abolished in America. Revival causes God's people to tackle moral issues head-on.

There's something else that happens. A great spiritual awakening affects the believer in his relationship with God. "Christians will," as one futurist said, "realize the consumer party is over." Revival stops the hoarding of wealth. God's people are ready to tithe their substance and themselves to His service, and funds are directed into the Lord's priorities. The church expands and marches forward when it becomes intense in its passion to hear from God.

Some people believe revival is like the wind, so uncertain that no one knows whether it is coming or going. They believe it is a special act of God that takes place once in every fifty years or so. But this is not the case. Revival reflects the church's standing with the Almighty, and He would like to see us in constant revival.

Spiritual renewal should be standard for the church. It is the only state compatible with the character and nature of God. He is ready, able and longing to send a great outpouring.

Here is the most important factor. *Revival is a direct result of prayer.* B.J. Willhite, author of *Why Pray?*, has risen every morning at 5:00 A.M. for thirty-five years to pray for several hours. When we pray, he says, we "set up the conditions under which God can legally impose His will in a given situation."

During my days at CBN we gathered every day at noon under Pat Robertson's leadership to pray for revival in our city and the world. Some days we prayed just thirty minutes, but on many occasions God's unusual presence caused us to remain in prayer one or two hours. I continued the same practice when Dayspring was formed. Revival is an *attitude* — a position desired by those who love God. "As the deer pants for the water brooks, so pants my soul for You, O God" (Ps. 42:1). Charles Finney once said, "It's hard to stray far away when you keep short accounts with God."

When the Holy Spirit has His rightful place of authority in the individual believer, revival fires begin to burn. It is only then we are ready to wage holy war on Satan's darkness. Revival is what signals the beginning of conquest.

There is one thing remaining for God's people to do. We must call on Him. "Call unto me, and I will answer thee, and show thee great and mighty things, which thou knowest not" (Jer. 33:3, KJV).

More than fifty years ago a tiny Indian mother prayed for her six sons and two daughters as they struggled to survive, living together in a single-room mud hut. One of the daughters died of starvation. But that young mother had found Christ as a little girl, and she cried out to God for her precious family and for her nation. She wore hard calluses on her knees from interceding. Often her children would find her caught away with God in prayer. Today all six sons are ministers of the gospel. Two of them are my closest associates in this effort to reach India. The prayers of my mother and their mother brought together sons of different races and tongues half a world apart. Now our hearts burn together for every village in India.

Don't wait for your church or your denomination to call for the windows of heaven to be opened. It begins with you! Again and again God has used one individual to change the course of history.

The Great Corridor

There's a region known in missions as "the 10/40 window." It may sound like a thermo-pane glass, but it is a corridor of geography stretching from West Africa's Ivory Coast across the burning sands of the Sahara, over the cold, mystic peaks of the Himalayas into the ancient land of China and beyond to Japan, between ten degrees north to forty degrees north of the equator. "Most of the unreached people groups live here," said Luis Bush, international president of Partners International in his address to the Lausanne II missions conference in Manila.

That window includes the "cradle of civilization" and 62 countries. The corridor is home to 700 million Moslems, 800 million Hindus and over 150 million Buddhists. The poorest of the poor live here. But, as Bush states, "only 8 percent of all missionaries work among these people."

Research, development, building programs, gathering statistics, analysis and philosophizing about missions are all important. Jesus, however, was not thinking about demographics or bricks and mortar when He said, "Go, and make disciples of all nations."

As the late Oswald J. Smith said in *The Challenge of Missions*:

> When Jesus left His disciples nearly two thousand years ago, He gave but one task: namely *world evangelism*. I can imagine Him talking to them something like this: "I am going to leave you, and I will be gone for a long time. While I am absent, I want you to do just one thing. Give this gospel of Mine to the entire world. See that every nation, tongue and tribe hears it."

Those were His instructions. That was the
one thing He told them to do, and they understood Him perfectly. But what has the church
done during the years He has been absent?
Have we carried out His orders. Have we
obeyed Him?

As a matter of fact, we have done everything else except the one and only thing He
told us to do. Jesus never told us to build
colleges, universities and seminaries, but we
have done it. He never told us to erect hospitals
and asylums and homes for the aged. He never
told us to build churches or to organize Sunday
schools and Youth For Christ rallies, but we
have done it. And we ought to have done it, for
it is all important and worthwhile.

But the one and only thing that He told us
to do is the one and only thing we have left
undone. We have not given His gospel to the
entire world. We have not carried out His
orders (used by permission of G.R. Welch
Company, Limited).

Those are strong words, but they are true. In fact, at
times the church has vigorously resisted Christ's final
instructions.

Trained theologian William Tyndale struggled to survive in a damp, dark, medieval prison at the base of the
castle of Vilvoorde in Oxford, England. He was translating the Bible into English, an act punishable by death
according to a law passed in England in 1408. Tyndale
dreamed of getting the Bible into the hands of the people — even the last plow boy. Early in October 1536
William Tyndale was taken out of the castle dungeon
across the moat and led to an open courtyard where

hundreds of people waited to watch his execution. He was tied to a stake and strangled to death, and then his body was burned to ashes in front of a cheering crowd. Tyndale's dying words were, "Lord, open the king of England's eyes."

Though the church resisted perhaps the greatest advance in its history, Tyndale's last prayer was answered a few months after his death when King James authorized the Bible to be translated into English and made available to the common people.

Over the centuries the church has been notorious for pious condemnation. It condemned the printing press, the translation of the Bible, the radio signal, motion pictures and television. It resisted missionaries like Hudson Taylor, who wanted to go to the interior of China. Today the church is reluctant to understand that twelve thousand unreached people groups still remain. The negative tendencies, however, must forever be buried. We must not resist contemporary methods of world evangelization.

God wants to ignite a passion for the souls of every tribe and nation on earth. It will become the most positive force the world has ever seen as it ushers in the return of His Son.

ELEVEN

THE GREAT
PRINCIPLES OF WAR

The lines of battle have been drawn.

We are involved in a conflict with far greater consequences than the Persian Gulf or a third World War. This is a final all-out invasion to liberate the souls of those who have been held captive by Satan and his legions. It's a war that must not be lost.

At this very hour the conflict rages. Nations are in upheaval. The "rulers of darkness in high places" are engulfing people everywhere — not only in Africa, China or the Middle East, but on the home front. The church has failed to grasp the enormity of the struggle, and we have become weak and defenseless in our own backyard.

In England over one thousand Muslim mosques have been built during the same period that six hundred Christian churches have closed. Buddhists, Hindus and Muslims are now spending millions to expand their beachhead on American soil.

Evangelism has been called "the unpaid debt of the church." We have failed to obey the direction of our Commander-in-Chief to bring the gospel to the nations. Now the world is invading the church. The New Age movement, neopaganism and cults are flourishing, and the front lines are no longer "over there."

Our mission in India, Africa and China cannot be completed without a total commitment to the struggle. The signal that was sent from a half-million Americans who joined forces at Washington for Jesus was only a starting point. Millions more must join the chorus of those who sang, "Onward Christian soldiers, marching as to war." I applaud men such as Larry Lea who is inviting people to join in a great prayer army and Dick Eastman for his "school of prayer" movement. But I know these men, and others like them, are not saying stay in your prayer closets but "pray as you go."

Some may have questioned the wisdom of Jesus when He commanded the disciples to "go into all the world and preach the gospel." Were the troops prepared? Was their strategy defined? Jesus emphasized the principle which too often Christian leaders stubbornly resist: *Going* is the most important point of the battle. We will never understand how to win until we join the fight.

My wonderful helpmate, Caroline, rebuked me in a loving way when she said, "You've talked and prayed long enough about this film concept. Go to India and do it!" Even though I didn't have all the answers, I appreciated the practical wisdom she gave. It was as much a word from God as I have ever received.

Whether our assignment is Madras, Manila or Miami, we must respond to the call. We cannot say, "We'll start when we are ready." The battle is raging on every side. It's not a mop-up operation in a few isolated locations.

You may look around and say, "Why should I join the conflict? There's not enough help. I feel as though I'm fighting all alone." Like Moses, you may say, "Lord, I can't speak!"

But that is not the case. Right by your side is all the protection and fire power you will ever need. Not only is God watching over you, but He has specifically sent His Spirit as a mighty force. At age eighteen, attending a missions conference in Lancaster, Pennsylvania, I heard a verse of Scripture for the first time that has now become a powerful force in my life: "But you shall receive power when the Holy Spirit has come upon you; and you shall be witnesses to Me in Jerusalem, and in all Judea and Samaria, and to the end of the earth" (Acts 1:8).

Jesus lived with His disciples for three years, teaching them as they went. In the thousands of hours they spent together, He gave them detailed instructions and then commissioned them into battle. When He departed, He did not leave them all alone — He kept His promise and sent His Spirit.

What the followers of Christ did in a few short years — empowered by the Holy Spirit — was astounding. In fact, the invasion of the church in the first century was nothing short of incredible.

Now, two thousand years later, we are in a campaign that requires the same commitment and involvement. Why were the early Christians so successful? They were on the move. Scripture tells us that the followers of Christ "went everywhere preaching the word" (Acts 8:4).

No force on earth has ever been as strong as the church of Jesus Christ when it is in action. Armchair evangelism is doomed to failure. We can't sit back waiting for the postman to bring us battlefield reports in Christian magazines and ministry newsletters. The victory belongs to those who, after being taught the principles of evangelism, actually go.

Every Sunday school, church, Christian school, Bible college and Christian university must become a spiritual "war college." The fundamentals of Spirit-led warfare must be taught. Churches need to be boot camps to prepare every believer for conflict — not just hospitals to care for the sick.

General Ferdinand Foch was the commander of the Allied armies during World War I. He wrote a classic book titled *Principles of War*. When I opened the pages of his volume on military strategy, I was amazed at the parallel with the struggles we face.

Foch admonished the rulers of the Allied nations, declaring they could not run an "armchair" war and that the citizens of the Allied nations could not afford to be ignorant of the "eternal principles of tactics in open warfare" if they ever hoped to repel the kaiser.

He raised the question, "Can the principles of war be taught?" The answer is an unqualified yes. Foch establishes clearly that fundamental to the waging of a successful battle campaign is the instruction and "character build-up" of the soldiers. Preparedness is a supreme factor for accomplishing victory. We've got to get ready here before we can be victorious "over there."

Some imagine themselves as great ministers of the gospel on the other side of the world, but back home they do nothing. What you are at home you will be over there. Let God make you a soul-winner here before you enter His vineyard elsewhere.

In the final analysis, many of the lessons of war can only be taught by doing. Foch emphasized the need for the field generals to be "confident and independent." They must be full of confidence and in full command.

Decades later military strategists concluded that a fundamental mistake of the Vietnam War was that so much of its control remained in Washington, D.C. The exact opposite was the case in Operation Desert Storm in 1991. Notice the difference in the outcomes of those two stuggles.

God has given you the authority to act on His behalf. Your line of communication is open for any additional instruction or support you may need. Every Christian is a field commander in this final battle.

The fundamentals of battle must be observed and the textbook strategies applied to the spiritual struggle. I have studied the writings of noted military leaders and found there are basic laws of conquest that are universal. Let me summarize them into what I call the Twelve Great Principles of War.

Principle Number One:
Have a Clear Objective

What is the object of the Christian mission? "Jesus came and spoke to them, saying...'make disciples of all the nations' " (Matt. 28:18-19).

It is only when you have a well-defined goal that there is a possibility of success. Once that happens, every action becomes co-related to the ultimate objective. When you wake up in the morning you don't have to say, "I wonder what I should do today?"

Every move you make will have a purpose behind it.

Time is not on our side. Every hour nearly six thousand people who have never met Jesus are dying. As the

Chinese warrior Sun Tzu reportedly said in 500 B.C., "In war then, let your great object be victory, not lengthy campaigns."

Right now scores of new leaders are being trained in India by our allies in ministry. Bobji is a good example. He was only nineteen when I met him twelve years ago. Since his conversion at the age of nine he has been trained for Christian leadership. Today he heads multiple enterprises in God's kingdom — including orphanages, a chicken farm, schools and our Dayspring office.

He has a clear objective. One day he said to me, "John, tell all the people we are working day and night without ceasing to win the souls."

Principle Number Two:
Believe in the Cause

We must see our task as the great vocation it is. Paul said, "I press toward the mark for the prize of the high calling of God in Christ Jesus" (Phil. 3:14, KJV).

Ask any military man to rank the elements responsible for victory, and he'll place "believing in the cause" near the top of the list. General Carl Von Clausewitz was a noted German commander in World War I who also wrote a book titled *Principles of War*. He stated, "The principles of the art of war are in themselves extremely simple and quite within the reach of sound common sense. The conduct of war itself is without doubt very difficult. The great difficulty is this: to remain faithful throughout to the principles we have laid down for ourselves."

Clausewitz added, "If the military leader is filled with high ambition and if he pursues his aims with audacity and strength of will, he will reach them in spite of all obstacles; while an ordinary person would have found in the condition of his army a sufficient excuse for giving in."

The winning of souls cannot be based on a scientific formula or a systematic plan. It must be a passion of the soul. As a military man once said when he saw his troops committed to the conflict, "A new kind of war has begun; the hearts of soldiers have become a new weapon."

There was a young couple in India who met and fell in love. With every day that passed their love for one another grew. But one day the young man suddenly interrupted the romance by asking five surprising questions. "If we were to get married, would you be willing to go where I go? Learn the language of the people? Live a very simple life-style? Let me spend most of my time in ministry? And would you become my partner in prayer?" As the young lady thought it over, she realized the heart of her love was not her own — it belonged to Jesus. She could see the real question she was facing didn't revolve around her love for this man but rather her love for her Lord. He was questioning her values. "Are you willing to put the Lord and His gospel ahead of all else?" "Yes" was her reply.

That man is one of Dayspring International's mobile film team leaders located in the worst criminal district of India — the state of Bihar — and his name is Jebukamar. Jebu and his wife and family reach out to the needy Bhojpuris tribe, where four out of five people are illiterate — and almost half are under the age of fourteen! The Gospel of Mark is the only Scripture that has been translated into their language, making the Bhojpuris tribe the most unevangelized tribe in all of India. Almost every day Jebu goes out with his Bible, riding his motorcycle across the countryside. He has several scars on his face to prove the numerous beatings he has taken. Once an angry man pointed a pistol to his head and told him to stop preaching the gospel. He told me, "We are not afraid to die for the gospel's sake." During one three-month period, more than twelve thousand souls came to Christ through Jebu's leadership.

We will never win the world for Christ by joining the campaign out of guilt, duty or obligation. Like Jebu, our actions must spring from a heart that is filled with love for our heavenly Father, whose compassion for the lost flows through us.

Caroline and I don't rise every morning wondering if we should continue the pursuit of indigenous film evangelism. We made that exciting decision long ago, and it has become our reason for being.

Principle Number Three:
Obey Your Commander-in-Chief

The real challenge facing the church is obedience. It's time to realize, however, that following the command of Christ is a joy, not a judgment.

The Lord has not asked you to enlist; He has commissioned you to serve. Can you get excited about an honor like that? He told the disciples, "Follow me." That wasn't a suggestion but rather a gentle command. He said, "If you love Me, keep My commandments" (John 14:15). Then He added, "He who has My commandments and keeps them, it is he who loves Me. And he who loves Me will be loved by My Father, and I will love him and manifest Myself to him" (v. 21). Going God's way is indeed a joyous journey.

God's army must never be filled with people who aren't fit for anything else. The Lord wants to pull back the curtain and give you a glimpse of the harvest field — to make the vision so clear that you say, "I'm ready to go."

On the dock of Bombay's harbor, in the shadow of the giant stone arch called the Gateway to India, the eighty-five-year-old father-in-law of my friend P.K. Rajhuns told us of his burden and vision for India. "My great God has allowed me to preach His glorious gospel in seven languages over the last forty years. As my precious wife lay dying she saw beautiful golden steps to heaven and Jesus coming to carry her home." He wiped the tears from his glowing face and added, "I want to join her, but I also want to keep telling my people about Jesus. If only my legs were not so weak." Bobby Pollard, one of our dear friends of Dayspring, was so moved he too wept. "I wish I could give him my legs," he said to me.

Now the purpose of the commandment is love from a pure heart, from a good conscience, and from sincere faith (1 Tim. 1:5).

It's inspiring to know that your Commander wants to talk directly to you, to give you precise instructions — and even more. "If you are willing and obedient, you shall eat the good of the land" (Is. 1:19).

Principle Number Four:
Be Prepared

Many people see the thousands of souls who are coming to Christ through film evangelism and yet fail to realize that a great deal of instruction is involved in the harvest. Every native team member is involved in a Bible training program and has been carefully prepared to do the work of an evangelist. They are a vital part of this great army that is invading Satan's territory.

For decades the Boy Scouts have used as their motto: "Be prepared." It's excellent advice. *There is a prepared place for a prepared person.*

A military strategist once said, "War must not be waged arbitrarily or blindly. It is more than a science. It is knowledge applied to actual life, the development of the original guiding thought in accordance with constant changes of events; it is the art of acting under the pressure of the most difficult circumstances."

As I was considering leaving CBN because of my burden for souls in developing nations, God said to me: "Make yourself an expert in missions. Study the harvest. Know who they are, where they are and how to reach them." If I had not done my best to master the topic, I most likely would not have recognized the opportunity for indigenous film evangelism.

The challenge we face also requires that we discard outdated methods. All too often yesterday's battle plan just won't work. If Plan A does not succeed, use Plan B.

In a world where knowledge is exploding and the globe is rapidly changing, we must not only get prepared but *stay prepared.*

Principle Number Five:
Assemble a Massive Force

There is strength in numbers. We will never complete the task of world evangelism with a handful of people. The invading force must number in the hundreds of thousands. The pattern we have established overseas now makes it possible for unlimited numbers of film teams to take the visual gospel to the people. The two obstacles we face are trained personnel and financial resources.

I believe a major reason there are not enough trained people — or available finances — is the ignorance of Christian leaders regarding the nature of the harvest field. I asked the pastor of a seven-hundred-member church, "Do you understand what I mean by 'unreached people groups'?"

His answer saddened me. "No. What is an unreached

people group?"

Is it any wonder we lack the people-power — and that the average giving to missions is only ten cents per week per Christian? Much more must be done.

Believers of every practice of faith and color must band together to overwhelm the strongholds of Satan. We must stop drawing circles around our group, our denomination, our strategy, excluding until only a few remain in many separate circles. We will never win the battle with a fragmented force. If we have only one Commander, it makes sense that we unite as one army.

Paul said, "Some indeed preach Christ even from envy and strife, and some also from good will: The former preach Christ from selfish ambition, not sincerely, supposing to add affliction to my chains; but the latter out of love, knowing that I am appointed for the defense of the gospel. What then? Only that in every way, whether in pretense or in truth, Christ is preached; and in this I rejoice, yes, and will rejoice" (Phil. 1:15-18).

Christians from every corner of the globe must answer the call. Jesus said, "The harvest truly is great, but the laborers are few; therefore pray the Lord of the harvest to send out laborers into His harvest" (Luke 10:2).

Notice that the call is for laborers — not lords over the harvest. We are to work side by side.

Principle Number Six:
Keep Your Forces Mobile

An effective fighting force is ready to strike at any moment. It anticipates the opportunity for seizing the victory. The attitude is both mental and physical.

In missions, transportation has transformed our ability to reach people with the gospel. Certainly there are areas in the Himalayas and in the tropical rain forests that are still remote. But with land rovers, power boats and helicopters, the journey is not the ordeal it once was. Now we are entering an age of even faster mobility with new sources of energy, lighter materials and new vehicle designs.

An army that loses its ability to maneuver — that digs in mentally, spiritually or physically — is headed for surrender; it cannot attack and cannot retreat. The harvest field requires God's army to be mobile.

Principle Number Seven:
Keep Your Troops Well-Supplied

It's been said that "an army moves on its stomach." That's why the first objective of a military offensive is to cut off the enemy's lines of supply. A hungry soldier is a defeated foe.

If evangelizing the world is the supreme task of the church — and it is — then it is no wonder the enemy marshals every possible force to cut the lines of supply. This is no time to stop giving to missions.

In the campaign for the lost, the church is like an armory, and our arsenal must remain well-stocked. We are fed by the Word and fortified with prayer. We are the army of the righteous One.

What is our battle gear? "Therefore take up the whole armor of God, that you may be able to withstand in the evil day, and having done all, to stand" (Eph. 6:13).

It should come as no surprise that Paul gives us the specifics. I like the Moffatt translation here: "So take God's armor, that you may be able to make a stand upon the evil day and hold your ground by overcoming all the foe. Hold your ground, tighten the belt of truth about your loins, wear integrity like as your coat of mail, and have your feet shod with the stability of the Gospel of peace;

above all, take faith as your shield, to enable you to quench all the fire-tipped darts flung by the evil one, put on salvation as your helmet, and take the Spirit as your sword (that is, the Word of God), praying at all times in the Spirit, with all manner of prayer and entreaty — be alive to that, attend to it unceasingly, interceding on behalf of all the saints and on my behalf also..." (Eph. 6:14-18).

There are thousands of native evangelists, pastors, teachers and workers who need supply from the storehouse to continue their gallant efforts on the front lines. Rick Seaward, pastor of a five-thousand-member church in Singapore, told me his church gave over $1 million to missions in a single year, but even more amazing was the fact that the per capita income of the church was about half that of an average church in the United States.

The armory must be open to the needs of weary soldiers. In many cases, however, fully armed warriors remain inside the armory — checking their armor, polishing, eating and sleeping, but never entering the battle alongside their comrades.

We who are strong must reinforce the soldiers who are tired from battle. We are the enabling force.

Principle Number Eight:
Concentrate Your Power

Every great military leader will tell you that warfare is most effective if you (1) use your entire force with the utmost energy and (2) concentrate your power. As one old general explained his amazing succession of victories, "I gits thar the firstest with the mostest."

The same principle is found throughout Scripture. Christ multiplied His army time after time: "The Lord appointed seventy others also, and sent them two by two before His face into every city and place where He Himself was about to go" (Luke 10:1). They walked in harmony because the place of agreement is the place of power.

Christ also told His disciples to band together when they prayed. "Again I say to you that if two of you agree on earth concerning anything that they ask, it will be done for them by My Father in heaven. For where two or three are gathered together in My name, I am there in the midst of them" (Matt. 18:19-20).

Caroline and I have discovered that the greatest demonstration of concentrated power is when we agree together in prayer. The greater the focus of power, the more dynamic the results.

Principle Number Nine:
Use the Element of Surprise

Invading enemy territory can be a risky venture.

Peter Prakasem had organized a film showing I was to attend in a Hindu village. I sat in a van, the sliding panel door open for us to see from beside the crowd. The screen was stretched between two fifteen-foot-high bamboo poles. All seemed well as Peter opened in prayer. He rolled the projector, but as the first color pictures splashed onto the screen, a group of angry Hindu youths surrounded Peter and the equipment.

"Stop this immediately, or we will break your equipment and beat you!" they shouted.

Peter bravely argued, "But we have permission to be here."

"Never mind," they said as they shoved Peter.

The crowd of about five hundred watched. Peter began packing the gear. As he neared the van, they reached to snatch the gear out of his hands. At first he put his body between the angry men and us, closing the door behind him. We told him to get in. He jumped in the van, and we drove off. Peter cried. I comforted him. "Brother, you put your body between us and that angry gang. Don't be ashamed."

"I would have taken the beatings if you had not been here, Brother John," he said. "I didn't want you to get hurt, so I left." Then he added with determination, "The devil won't get the victory — we will go to another place without permission and show the film." We drove about thirty minutes and set up the equipment on a hilltop. People came running from everywhere to see Jesus.

Many of our film team members have been beaten because of their boldness in presenting the gospel. When we enter a village that is entirely non-Christian, the peril is high. That's why we often use the element of surprise. To thwart opposition against us, we often wait until the last possible moment to announce the film showing and set up the projector and screen.

The reality we face is far different from the times when, as a boy, my brother and I would play church. This is spiritual warfare, and we must employ every tactic at our disposal.

There is no time to waste. Satan is vulnerable, and he knows it. We need to attack him without warning. I can almost see him scurrying from the villages where Christ is presented on the screen. Even the audiences are taken by surprise. They've never heard or seen the story of Jesus. When He dies on the cross, it's as if the people want to walk up to the screen and take Him down. "How could they do that to someone who has done no wrong?" they ask.

Many great battles have been won — even when the invading force was outnumbered — because of the element of surprise. Gideon's army proved it. The shock of sudden ambush can quickly rout the enemy. The demons of hell tremble with fear wondering where the next thrust of mass evangelism will appear.

Principle Number Ten:
Take Decisive Action

It's been said, "He who hesitates is lost." Victory requires positive, determined action. Completing the task of world evangelism requires the same tactic. As one preacher said, "Go straight at them with the gospel."

We will never defeat the enemy with hit-and-run tactics. We're not playing hide and seek with Satan. Instead, we must take aim directly on our foe and strike with such strong and sustained force that he never has a chance to regroup.

We can't delay the moment of truth. You'll never have a victory without a battle. Presenting Christ on the big screen to the unreached people of the world started with just a flicker, but the light is now destroying the darkness with growing intensity. Our task is clear, and our actions are decisive. As Paul wrote, "I determined not to know anything among you except Jesus Christ, and Him crucified" (1 Cor. 2:2).

A military leader once commented, "Victory is the price of blood." As Christians we have known that since the moment of our salvation. Christ died not only for our sin, but for the sin of the entire world.

Principle Number Eleven:
Stay on the Offensive

A major reason that military tacticians like to keep their armies on the move is so they are in a position to attack. Foxholes (including Bible studies, prayer meetings, seminars and conferences) serve their purpose, but you certainly don't want to stay in them too long. Once the enemy targets your location, you're suddenly fighting to save your life, not to conquer your foe.

In our ministry I have realized that the greatest resistance comes from within the church, not from the world. In India people are being converted literally by the millions, but when I return I must listen to those who say, "Don't you think it's wrong to have a native of India playing the part of Jesus?"

Fortunately, I've learned to smile and pray that someday, some way, they will get to see firsthand "the fields white unto harvest" and that they will become culturally sensitive to the needs of others.

Christ has never had to defend the Great Commission. From the moment He uttered those words, a committed corps of believers has accepted it, and many have turned the world "upside down." They went on the offensive.

Proclaiming the death, burial and resurrection of Jesus to lost humanity will produce enough persecution to keep our doctrine pure and our swords sharp. It is when we have time on our hands that we lose our cutting edge.

The gospel is by its very nature offensive. The term is not used to indicate that we are to be insulting or rude, but aggressive. When the message is preached, it's the recipient who is suddenly on the defensive. They must make a decision.

Over and over in the villages of India we see former idol worshippers repent and claim Jesus as their *only* Lord. Just watching the film is enough for hundreds in each audience to be born again.

Christ is a Lord of action. People respond to Him because He touches their lives through healing, through love and through salvation.

Principle Number Twelve:
See the Victory As Already Won

If you plan to win, you must see yourself winning. Behavioral research has proven that theory repeatedly. As Christians, however, we don't have merely to think we have overcome the enemy; we know from Scripture it is true.

It is thrilling to know that the Lord goes before us. It's a fact. His name is Jehovah Nissi — "our banner." He is also Jehovah Jireh — "the one who sees ahead and makes provision."

When Christ said on the cross, "It is finished," Satan became a defeated foe. It was at that point that freedom became ours. "Therefore if the Son makes you free, you shall be free indeed" (John 8:36). He is our righteousness and our peace.

Now is the time to claim the promise of the Word. "You are of God, little children, and have overcome them, because He who is in you is greater than he who is in the world" (1 John 4:4).

The Christ we are presenting to the world is the righteous Judge who has destroyed the enemy. He said, "I will build My church, and the gates of Hades shall not prevail against it" (Matt. 16:18).

When a villager gazes at the screen, he sees a triumphant Lord who destroys death, sets the captives free and shakes the bonds of earth to ascend to His Father. "O grave, where is thy victory?" The victory has been won!

In his book *Megatrends*, John Naisbitt said, "At the dawn of the third millennium there are unmistakable signs of a worldwide multidenominational religious revival."

When we who are believers look back at this time from the windows of eternity, we will see the Holy Spirit fire descending on continent after continent. We will behold those who with clarity of objective believed in the cause. They obeyed the Commander, prepared themselves, joined each other in unity, kept on the move, supplied the need, focused their power, used surprise, took decisive action, kept on the offensive and always envisioned the victory.

I firmly believe and many others believe that the mighty nations will have fallen. China will be democratized and a Christian nation. Africa will be one of the greatest continents for Christ on earth. The strongholds of Satan — Hinduism, Islam, Buddhism, animism and the New Age — will all be in shambles. Millions from Europe, South America, Africa, Asia and the Middle East will bow in praise and worship to the One who said to His disciples, "All authority has been given to Me in heaven and on earth. Go therefore and make disciples of all nations, baptizing them in the name of the Father and of the Son and of the Holy Spirit" (Matt. 28:18b-19).

God's great principles of war allow no room for defeat. The final celebration is about to begin. An innumerable host is being gathered out of every kindred, tribe and tongue.

TWELVE

PICK UP THE SWORD!

I'm going to ride my bike now, Dad," said our youngest son, Stephen.

He was about seven years old at the time, and we had been working together in the garage on a small "father and son" carpentry project. He'd been helping me by hammering nails into some wood. When he grew weary of banging on the board, he looked up at me — his red hair sticking out from under his baseball cap — and announced that he was going to ride his bicycle.

As I continued to work, suddenly there was a commotion. I looked around to see Stephen struggling to pull his bike through the door over a foot-high threshold. He'd managed to get the front wheel across, but it was now straddled, and he couldn't lift it any farther.

I thought I would surprise him, so as he continued to pull and struggle I gently lifted the bike up by the back of the seat, and it moved forward over the threshold. Stephen never looked back but continued on out the door as if he had done the job all alone.

I walked outside and asked, "Stephen, do you know what happened back there?"

"No," he said, "I was just having a hard time getting my bike out of the door."

"Well, how did you do it?"

"I don't know," he said. "It just went over all of a sudden."

"Stephen, I want you to listen to me very carefully," I told him. "It's something I don't want you to forget. I came up behind you and put my hand under the bicycle seat and gently lifted it up to help you across. You didn't even know I was there. Stephen, that's the way God helps Daddy. He does it all the time, even though I don't know He's there." My little freckled-face boy smiled and rode off on his bicycle. I returned to my carpentry with a profound sense of comfort knowing that my heavenly Father was observing me through all my struggles and lifting me over them.

The challenges we face, however, are insignificant when compared with the great work God has called us to do. In fulfilling the Great Commission, we are representatives of the King of kings.

The Ambassador's Club

The noisy Bombay airport lobby was crowded. I had been traveling for nearly forty hours and was at the point of total exhaustion.

"Can't we find a place to rest?" I said to my Indian friend at the air terminal in India's largest city.

"No," he said. "I've looked everywhere. There's not a seat to be found. And if we go outside, we'll be bothered by beggars."

Then he said, "Oh, there is one place, but it's only for very important people. You've got to be a member of a special club and have a registration pass. But let's go over and see what they will do."

As we approached the special room, there was a uniformed guard standing at the door. He had a gun.

"May I help you?" said the guard.

My Indian friend said, "We'd like to come in."

"Well, who are you?" he replied.

I just knew he was going to tell the man we were missionaries or preachers, and the guard would chase us away.

My friend leaned forward and whispered confidently to the man, "Sir, we are ambassadors of the most high God."

The officer straightened up, whipped open the door and said, "Oh, please come in!" We had a rest, were served refreshments and were treated like royalty.

In fulfilling God's great vision, there are times when the reception is not so cordial. William Carey was rebuked when he shared his missionary burden with his sponsoring church in England. But still he translated the Bible into thirty-four Indian languages and is today called the father of modern missions. Hudson Taylor was not a brilliant intellectual or dynamic public personality, but the vision God gave him for China was greater than any obstacle. Over six thousand missionaries joined him in the great cause.

In India, where native leaders were at first skeptical

that a dramatic film could establish churches, there has been a revolution in strategy. Mission leaders who once said, "It will never work," are calling to say, "John, it is really possible. We can reach all the villages of India." Pat Robertson echoed those words when he told me, "If you continue on this present course, all of the great nation of India can be evangelized."

Now, when I pray, the words are not, "Lord, help me launch another film team in India." Instead I am saying, "Lord, help us mobilize several thousand film teams to every continent."

At times I have to pinch myself to realize I'm not just seeing another vision on a wall. It's real! Millions right now are coming to Christ, and I am convinced God is going to use the exact same method to reach the remaining nations — the "hidden peoples" of the world. Like an ocean it will flood the world with God's mercy and usher in the return of our Lord.

"We've Got to Do Something, Daddy"

I was in the middle of my sermon when suddenly my son John — he was just five years old at the time — ran to the altar. His big blue eyes flowed with tears as he knelt in prayer.

It was a typical church service. I brought John with me because I wanted to be with my boys as much as possible. He was seated about eight rows back on the center aisle. I could see his disheveled blond hair and glistening eyes just above the pew in front of him. John liked to draw, but tonight he was very attentive as I spoke to the congregation of about two hundred.

I was startled when, without an invitation, John slid off his seat and ran down the aisle, dropped to his knees and cried, "We've got to do something, Daddy. We've got to help these people." His body shook as he sobbed.

The entire audience was surprised. But I was sensitive enough to realize this was no emotional outburst. God was exhorting me that the Holy Spirit was speaking through the innocent lips of a child.

I stepped down to the altar rail where John knelt, and I embraced him. Then I looked up to the audience and, without finishing my message, gave an invitation. From all over that sanctuary they came — some solemn, some weeping. Others knelt at their pew. God met us in an unusual manner. His voice that night was that of a young boy whose body, soul and spirit spoke the true essence and nature of this gospel we love to proclaim. "We've got to do something, Daddy. We've got to help these people."

One of Satan's greatest ploys to defeat us is to delude us into thinking we should be "silent witnesses," not making a disturbance with the message of the gospel. But the Word must be spoken to the lost. "How shall they hear without a speaker or preacher?" (see Rom. 10:14). Someone must be the vocal chords and lips of the gospel. There is no option to remain silent. We've got to do something.

Our goal at Dayspring International is to mobilize one million Christians into a force for the Great Commission such as the world has never known. For years the church has centered its attention on self-help training and personal development — teaching everything from stress reduction to the secret of effective prayer. That same energy must now be transformed into a massive effort on behalf of missions. Just as Christians have been inspired to build theme parks, television stations, conference centers and retirement villages, the time has arrived for the whole church to become excited about evangelizing the whole world.

Our goal is clear. We are committed to seeing the gospel visualized for the whole world. Our team is currently making plans for major film productions of the life of Christ for every major culture. Each of these films will have an all-indigenous cast and will be shot on location. Would it not be wonderful if a million Christians made a commitment to see this done in their lifetime? And these films will evangelize until Jesus comes whether that is within one year or fifty.

A Black Jesus?

If you were to visit the Easter pageant of a black Baptist church in East St. Louis, what color would Jesus be? If you watched a Christmas drama in Nairobi, Kenya, what color would the baby Jesus in the manger be?

I believe God gave His Son for the whole world. The color of His skin or His facial features are insignificant when it comes to the message of His birth, death and resurrection. You can be saved without knowing His race or the village where He was born. All you need to know is that Christ died for your sins.

The power of an all-native cast presenting the life of Christ on film is incredible. No foreign-made film can come close to its effectiveness.

In Nigeria nationals are pleading with us to duplicate what has been done in India. The co-chairman of our African steering committee, Mac O. Nwulu, already knows the power of film. Recently twenty-seven citywide film festivals were held showing American-made Christian movies. Total attendance was 860,000, and 319,000 were won to Christ. Says Nwulu, "The moment we have an African life of Christ [film] we will win millions upon millions to the Lord."

Without question I believe this will be the answer to the chief of the Zulu tribe who pleaded, "Come and tell our people about Jesus." Think of it! A black Jesus looking down from the cross.

Commission China

Our plans for a major all-Chinese life of Christ film will have the same impact. The production company is formed; the script is written; the director has been chosen. A key Chinese Christian church and business leaders have met and unanimously committed themselves to this strategy to touch the nations of the Pacific rim. As one pastor put it, "This is not a project; this is a lifeline to 1.2 billion people who need Jesus Christ."

Our research concerning the film industry in China indicates that we will reach hundreds of millions in theaters, while official government film teams will take it to the villages. Over twenty-one *billion* tickets were sold to movies in China in 1990. We believe the national television networks in China will also be available. What about government regulations? The message of Christ is not at odds with national policy. They can certainly identify with the Lord when He says, "If you want to be perfect, go, sell what you have and give to the poor, and you will have treasure in heaven; and come, follow Me" (Matt. 19:21). We are victorious!

When *Oceans of Mercy* was shown to the censorship committee of the Indian government — mostly Hindus — they gave their approval without stipulations. They found nothing offensive about the film. They believed that Jesus was a wonderful character who identified with people, would uplift their spirits and give them joy and happiness. Though our adviser in Beijing says this film subject is so sensitive that only the premier himself can give the final approval, I believe God will go before us and the premier's heart will be touched by prayer.

As in India, the follow-up efforts in new nations are

designed to disciple converts and establish Christian churches without regard to denomination.

Additionally, there is a great need for feature-length animated films to reach the children of the world. A classic such as John Bunyan's *The Holy War* is a universal communicator of the gospel. It passes the "culture test" and can be dubbed into every language. Our goal is to complete production by the end of the decade. It will be the most powerful dramatic piece of animation ever conceived. It will employ the finest talent and latest computer graphic capabilities. Audiences will be astounded with truth in a twenty-first-century format.

Living in the Future

Another major objective is to make the Great Commission do-able. We want to be the enabling force that says, How can we help you? For example, we recently sponsored a training program for fifteen hundred Indian pastors. We gave them materials in their own language — including a Bible with a concordance and study helps they'd never had before. A conference for ten thousand pastors is planned next.

Fortunately, we are not starting from scratch. Dayspring is standing on the shoulders of pioneer missions organizations and indigenous ministries which have accomplished great works. But now we must provide massive amounts of Christian materials for the follow-up effort, which includes discipling, training of Christian workers and church building. It is here that literature, video and other products are needed.

We cannot afford to confine our thinking to the present if whole nations are to be discipled. Like most giant corporations, IBM has a twenty-year plan. Multinational enterprises pour tens of millions into research and development. Today products are being tested that will not be sold for five or ten years. As one executive told me, "We live in the future and pull the population with us."

I am inspired and yet grieved when I read the history of global industrial giants like Coca-Cola that have penetrated world markets in a manner never thought possible. You can purchase American soft drinks in practically every nation of the world. American cigarettes are promoted on giant billboards throughout emerging nations. Even Mickey Mouse has enormous international fame. Names like Mohammed Ali, the Beatles and Arnold Schwarzenegger are known by hundreds of millions of people in every continent. Why? Because of savvy marketing and control of the media.

Today's technology must be used creatively to reach the world for Christ — everything from handheld super computers, fiber-optic phone lines carrying ten million phone calls at a time and personal helicopter cars. A member of our staff recently met with the Sony Corporation regarding development of a solar-powered CD Rom library that would revolutionize Bible training for village pastors. It is possible with the present hardware and software to present a native pastor with one small unit that contains hundreds of the world's greatest Christian resources — from Bible commentaries to training courses and even learning-to-read programs.

Why should ministers in North America and Europe have unlimited resources, from laptop computers to fax machines, while those laboring among the hundreds of millions of unreached people have virtually nothing? They barely have the pages of God's Word available in their own language — and over three thousand languages have not been translated. I cry with the late Cam Townsend, founder of Wycliffe, "Lord, it ought not to be." The amazing thing is we *can* do something about it, and that is part of our vision.

Why hasn't the church penetrated the world with the message of Christ? In our efforts to become catalysts for global evangelism it has become evident that, with few exceptions, there is not a commitment to research and development on the part of the church. Thank God for organizations such as the U.S. Center for World Mission, and people such as David Barrett who is research consultant to the foreign mission board of the Southern Baptist Convention. They have taken on the enormous challenge of providing information and analysis of world conditions and the development of strategies for missions. The church, however, is failing to use this information aggressively to reach the nations. I interviewed twenty of the world's leading future thinkers at a conference on the future. The gospel of Jesus Christ was not a factor in their consideration. However, they all agreed religion's influence on the world of tomorrow was a big factor. The workshop on religion was jam-packed. Why? Because man's search for truth is real. Jesus Christ is that truth, but we have failed to tell them.

At times I have felt like "a voice crying in the wilderness" regarding the awesome power of indigenous film evangelism. I am shocked when I read books by leading missiologists and strategists on accomplishing the Great Commission. One of the most popular current books on world evangelism has a great deal to say about the use of radio and literature, but just two small sentences on the use of film. Yet the motion picture we are using in India is bringing more souls into the kingdom than any method in the history of missions in that nation.

It Works!

The indigenous film concept of the life of Christ is a

major strategy for reaching the world. While many people are wondering what can be done, we are presenting the gospel to over one million people every month. The advantages of a cinematic presentation of the gospel are that the message is always consistent, it never gets tired or forgetful, it is always dramatic and it is in color — with music. It holds the audience's undivided attention for over two and a half hours.

Is it worth the effort? The results thus far say that it is. We have already reached over thirty million people in India with *Oceans of Mercy*. Over three million have accepted Christ as their Savior, and hundreds of churches have been established. Before missionary Mark Buntain died, he said, "This film can do more to reach India's millions for Christ than all other past efforts combined."

That's a bold statement from a man who gave thirty years of his life in Calcutta.

Vijayan Pavamani, a member of the Lausanne Committee for World Evangelization, says, "We have been praying for a way to reach the masses of India. This film makes it possible."

Joe Umidi, a professor at Regent University, went to India to see it firsthand. "I watched the film being shown on the campus of a Hindu school and was deeply moved by the hundreds of men and women who received Christ as their Savior that night. This is the best method of Third World evangelism I know of."

The cost of producing and distributing a major motion picture of the life of Christ with an all-native cast is not cheap. The results, however, show that it is cost-effective and worth every dollar invested. Where will the money come from? I believe that people with resources are going to step forward. God is preparing businessmen and investment groups which will be formed to fund a commercially viable product that — just as in India — can be shown in theaters to recoup the cost. Then copies of the film can be placed in the hands of national film teams to reach the villages. It can be done in Rio de Janeiro, Beijing, Manila, Tokyo, Seoul, Nairobi — and, yes, even in Tel Aviv or Baghdad.

Ernest and Vijay

My meeting with Ernest Komanapalli at the home of an Indian family in Virginia Beach was providential. In addition to providing leadership for Dayspring International in India, he has led his own ministry which has grown to include over seven hundred churches and pastors, two hospitals, thirty-five orphanages, several Bible colleges and a high school with nearly one thousand students.

What about Vijay Chandar? From the moment I first met the Hindu film actor and producer at the Madras airport in 1979, it was obvious that God's hand was guiding his life. The same Lord who wouldn't let him stop making the film when all odds were against him is the same Lord who has entered into his heart.

The transformation has been complete. In 1990 we invited Vijay to Dayspring International headquarters in Virginia Beach to meet with our staff and plan future film productions. As a result of a personal encounter with the One who gives unmerited mercy, Vijay made a commitment to present his talents to the Lord. "John," he told me, "from this moment forward I will produce nothing but films which honor Christ."

Things to Come

So often I am now asked, "John, what does the future hold for world evangelism? What is on the horizon?"

Since my first journey to Asia, an epic event has taken place. It was written about in the book *Pacific Rising* by Simon Winchester. He said on May 4, 1984, for the first time in history more jumbo jets flew over the Pacific Ocean than the Atlantic — and the rate is ever-increasing. He calls the jumbo jet "one of the most potent symbols of this century." His book tells a dramatic story of the shift of power and influence to the Pacific Rim.

Winchester says there is a "new center of the world economically, politically, socially and spiritually." It is the Pacific Ocean, around which some fifty countries group. History shows us that world leadership has shifted from the Mediterranean, to the Atlantic and now to the Pacific.

What many Christians may not have considered is that the religious philosophies of these people are older than Christianity and will play a greater role in the twenty-first century.

Already Western businessmen must study the philosophy of Confucius and the religious tenets of Buddhism in order to be capable of communication with their Pacific Rim counterparts.

The United States has already been labeled a post-Christian society. Is it so because the church failed to reach out to the world? Is it because we Americanized the gospel so much that it could not be received?

What irony to see the atheistic Soviet Union fling open its doors to religious liberty while the most blessed nation on earth seems to turn its back on God.

Where is the world's largest church? It is Paul Yonggi Cho's church in Korea. Where is the fastest-growing church? Sumba, Indonesia — it doubled to 150,000 in just two years. What continent may soon be more Christian than North America? Africa.

As we enter the greatest century since the birth of

Christ, it is ironic that Pacific Rim nations may have to be evangelized by missionaries from Africa, Korea, South America and China. And America may also have to be brought back to God by missionaries from the Pacific Rim.

Asia is exploding with gospel fervor. I spoke in Singapore to Calvary Center's audience of some four thousand people on a Sunday evening. I talked about our desire to reach the Chinese people with a motion picture of the life of Christ played by all Chinese actors. Calvary sponsors three hundred full-time missionaries and has birthed more than fifty dynamic churches throughout the world. Yet, when I gave an invitation for people to give their lives to missions, hundreds more rushed forward to the altar. The pastor, George EE, led the congregation in a stirring prayer of commitment unlike anything I have ever heard in America. The Holy Spirit is sweeping across Asia. It is awesome to see.

I met with thirty of Africa's key Christian leaders to discuss the production of an all-African, life-of-Jesus film. Their response was an overwhelming mandate to do it quickly. More astounding was their belief that the funding of the film could and should come primarily from the African people. The leaders declared: "This will be the most powerful tool of evangelism we have ever used."

The sleeping giant of evangelism — indigenous motion pictures on the life of Christ — is being awakened to enable the church to fulfill the Great Commission more effectively.

One futurist author wrote, "Tomorrow will surprise us all." But I believe tomorrow must be molded by the proclamation of the gospel to the world groping for truth. The message of Christ is the only hope for a world being torn apart by disintegrating governments, collapsing economies and societal ills. Emerging nations are being consumed by consumerism. It is predicted that by 2015 A.D. over 100 million people will die in Africa because of AIDS. It's been described as absolute genocide. A similar epidemic is descending on Asia. Are we our brothers' keepers? Do we not *owe* them the gospel? Every Christian should say *yes*.

Passing the Baton

In 1990 Donald McGavran, perhaps this century's greatest missions strategist, spoke to me directly from his heart. He was suffering from bone cancer and died a few weeks later at the age of ninety-four. Born in India of missionary parents, he returned there as a third-generation missionary himself in 1923. He founded the School of World Missions at Fuller Theological Seminary and was the author of many influential books.

I asked him, "What is the last word you would want to say to me and to others as you pass the baton and prepare to step into the presence of the Lord?"

His answer was: "The priority of evangelism must be the planting of the church in every ethnic group. The church has yet to see the great importance of this strategy in fulfilling God's will. I believe the next stage is to make entire ethnic groups disciples of Jesus rather than reaching only individuals." McGavran believed that the goal of Christian missions should be to plant a "cluster of growing congregations" in every segment of the world's population.

He later continued his answer in a letter. He started by explaining the original Greek words that make up the Great Commission: *matheteusate panta ta ethne*.

What the Great Commission really says is, "Incorporate into My body, the church, all segments of society everywhere." This includes all the tribes of the earth, all the clans, all the distinguishable homogenous units of the vast populations of mankind, all the castes, the educated, the uneducated, the poor, the rich, the heavily dressed Eskimos and the very scantily dressed Africans living along the equator at sea level.

What you need to say in a very clear way — and what I want to say through you — is that the Lord Jesus Christ Himself commanded all of us Christians to proclaim the gospel in the languages of the people and the culture of the people, knowing the religion of the people so that those who are now worshipping idols, images, human ideas and many other forms of man-made false gods will abandon them and come to worship the one true God.

This is a huge task, and you and I need to carry it out. As I lay down Christ's sword, you pick it up and insist that all other Christians pick it up.

With every day that passes it is clear that our mission is much more than simply presenting a film and seeing thousands of people make decisions for Christ. We must offer it in such a way as to make disciples of entire groups, even nations of people. Counting converts, as exhilarating as it may be, is not the answer. Discipling is our commission.

McGavran's words still ring in my ears: "Pick up the sword! Pick up the sword!"

Rescued on the Sea

My heart continues to burn with the same passion I experienced the first time I saw people respond to *Daya Sagar*. Since that day millions more have seen His glory. They have witnessed the Man of great redemption who came to put His arm around a leper and save the most wretched sinner. Those who were blind could now see.

I can still hear the Lord saying to me, "I want you to do the same thing I did when I was on earth. I spoke to the people in parables and stories. I want you to do the same thing."

As a result of the Lord's clear direction, I embarked on my journey.

When Mr. Phillips came to my home and placed ten dollars in my hand, he had no idea how it would be multiplied. He could only see a teenager who loved the Lord, but God could see a harvest of souls.

God doesn't call everyone to sell his or her home and launch a global ministry. He has, however, called you and me to fulfill the Great Commission. Some go in person, others with their finances and others with their prayers.

In villages across India tonight thousands will gather for the start of another presentation of the life of Christ. My mother will be there. Her prayers were sent ahead long, long ago. They are part of a chain of events that will lead to the day when God calls His people home from every tribe and nation.

So often I think about the words of the hymn by G.T. Haywood, "I see a crimson stream of blood. It flows from Calvary." At first the stream was but a trickle. Then it became a river. Now it has become a mighty sea.

Tonight, after the projector has been silenced and the screen is dim, a native film team member will throw out a life raft to people who have been drowning in their sin.

"THEY'RE KILLING AN INNOCENT MAN!"

Many will be rescued because of *Daya Sagar — Oceans of Mercy*.

COMMISSION
WORLD

Israeli jets in practice formation roared across the valley of Megiddo as I watched from the top of the mound where King Solomon's famed horse stables stood nearly three thousand years earlier. A gentle breeze rippled green waves of tall grass over the plains to the mountains beyond, where interpreters of prophecy believe hordes of mighty warriors will descend on Israel to devour her.

During my life, volumes upon volumes have been written about Armageddon, that final conflict, the war to end all wars. I confess the subject lost my attention quickly as my eyes turned to see another field — that field "white unto harvest." Is it wrong to believe that Christians do not need to be overly concerned about a battle that is most surely the Lord's? Is it not time to focus instead on the one true priority? Just hours after conquering death, hell and the grave and only a few days before His ascension, Jesus gave His disciples the Great Commission to preach the gospel to the world.

Can we in this generation look for that blessed hope of His return not so we can be snatched out of the tribulation but in order that we may present Him a glorious bride? As my thoughts return to the sight of Armageddon, I find myself praying, "O Lord, save us from any more diversions. Pour out a revival of love for all nations. Mark this decade with a new Pentecost. Prevent another generation from wasting tens of millions of man hours arguing about the future while forgetting the needs of the lost today."

The awesome battle Christians everywhere face is not Armageddon, but the war Satan has waged against them to keep them from understanding their glorious call to go into all the world on behalf of their Savior.

In chapter 12 I raised this question: What if there were one million Christians who would bind together to fulfill the Great Commission in their lifetimes? I would like to expand on that idea briefly. If one million agreed in prayer concerning the specific fulfillment of the Great Commission, would it become a reality? If one million gave of their time to bring in the harvest — if just one million committed their resources systematically to specific programs over a sustained period, would it not happen? What then must we do?

I believe God will call one million people who will covenant to proclaim Jesus Christ and Him crucified in a culturally relevant manner as outlined in this book.

By virtue of the fact that this book is in your hands, could it not be that you are one of the million whom God is calling?

After laboring in India for more than a decade, God has given Dayspring a global vision, and so Commission World has come into being. Commission Africa and Commission China are rapidly becoming reality, and in the near future other major cultural megaspheres will be targeted for this global strategy. Ten years ago this would have been a faraway dream. Today it is happening.

Should you not be informed of the progress being made to produce the story of Jesus for the major cultures of the world? If you would like to receive more information, please write Dayspring International, P.O. Box 3309, Virginia Beach, Virginia 23454.

Days before this book went to press, I was in Galilee. I climbed a hill overlooking the sea where Jesus did so many marvelous works. Was it on this hill or perhaps one very near that Jesus stood before His disciples in resurrection glory and gae them His final instructions? Could it be that this, our generation, may see those words fulfilled? I breathed a prayer: "Even so, come quickly, Lord Jesus."

As followers and ambassadors of Jesus Christ, we can work together to fulfill the Lord's command from the Great Commission: *mathetuesate panta ta enthne* — incorporate into My body, the church, all segments of society everywhere.